Soups & Sandwiches

by
Sue & Bill Deeming

HPBooks

ANOTHER BEST-SELLING VOLUME FROM HPBOOKS

Publishers: Bill and Helen Fisher; Executive Editor: Rick Bailey;
Editorial Director: Helen Fisher; Editors: Veronica Durie, Faye Levy;
Art Director: Don Burton; Book Design: Dana Martin;
Food Stylists: Janet Pittman, Sue Deeming; Photography: George de Gennaro Studios

Published by HPBooks
P.O. Box 5367, Tucson, AZ 85703 602/888-2150
ISBN 0-89586-216-6
Library of Congress Catalog Card Number 83-80967
© 1983 Fisher Publishing Inc. Printed in U.S.A.

The authors wish to thank the following for providing accessories used in the photography: Corning Glass Works; General Electric; Commercial Aluminum Cookware (manufacturers of Calphalon cookware); Schiller & Asmus, Inc. (importers of Le Creuset cookware); The Foley Company; Leyse Aluminum Company; Global Distributors (importers of Guzzini kitchenware).

COVER PHOTO: Minestrone, page 128, and Sandwich Loaf Italiano, page 81.

Contents

Soup & Sandwich—A Perfect Pair

Soups and sandwiches, served separately or combined, are usually thought of as an easy lunch or late supper. They can be hot and hearty or cold and delicate. What better food to warm freezing skiers than a steaming bowl of soup? What pleases a teenager more than a stack of cold-cuts, cheese and pickles on rye? With such benefits, why limit their use to lunch or supper. Soups and sandwiches fit any meal.

Feature a soup, sandwich or combination for breakfast, lunch or dinner. For breakfast, replace ready-to-eat cereal with refreshing cold fruit soup made in a blender, or hot, delicious Bacon & Egg Chowder. Sandwiches make great eye-openers for late risers who eat on the run. Serving a soup or sandwich for dinner does not necessarily make it an informal meal. Seafood specialties such as Russian Chlodnik—a creamy shrimp and beet mixture—make an elegant dinner.

As appetizers, soups and sandwiches stimulate the taste buds for the meal that follows. When there is room for dessert, a light fruit-and-wine soup or regal layered meringue-and-cream sandwich is a delicate ending.

Soups and sandwiches are truly versatile foods, and belong on the table any time. Suggestions for menus using them are given throughout the book. You can create meals with soups and sandwiches in a variety of ways. Many recipes can be meals by themselves. Half-servings of either soup or sandwich make a lighter meal. The sandwich-bread recipes provide another possibility. Buttered fresh bread with a hearty bowl of soup makes an ideal lunch or supper.

In addition to the hearty sandwich fillings you'll find throughout the book, Sandwich Spreads can be used by themselves as simple but tasty fillings. Or, use them to give subtle added flavor to your favorite sandwiches. ෯

The Story of Soups

The origins of soup are untraceable. References to soup have been found as early as 2000 B.C. Soup was known to ancient Greeks and Romans, Mayan Indians, North American Indians and Eskimos. The world's people have enjoyed soup through the ages.

Soup probably began with the invention of a heat-resistant bowl or pot. Whatever ingredients were on hand could be combined in the pot with water, then set over the fire. Cooked in this manner, food did not have to be constantly watched and turned.

Throughout its history, soup has been a simple food, except for the lavishly rich soups served to kings. Common people made soup from leftovers or small amounts of food not worth cooking any other way. The soup pot might simmer next to the fire or on the back of the stove all day.

Today's soup is a sophisticated food. Its flavor is purposely developed. Fresh ingredients are added to achieve a desired taste. A few soups are simmered for hours, but most are only cooked until flavors blend for a distinctly delicious taste.

Soup is convenient and economical. A hearty soup can be a one-dish meal, saving preparation of other foods. Most soups cook in about an hour. Quick soups are ready to serve in 20 minutes or less. Soups are budget-stretchers because the broth carries the flavor of all the ingredients. Even the most expensive ingredients can be spread out among many servings without loss of flavor. Soups are simmered on top of the stove. Thus, energy costs are much lower than cooking in an oven. Some soups can be prepared in a slow cooker or pressure cooker using even less energy.

Healing powers have been attributed to soups. Throughout time, mothers have used chicken soup to cure colds, flu and whatever ails their offspring. Though not possessing magical powers, soup is nutritious food. Nutrients are not lost in discarded cooking liquid.

Research is showing that soup is ideal for those who are weight-conscious. Because it is a liquid, soup must be eaten with a spoon and that takes time. Extra time aids digestion and helps prevent overeating. A meal of soup is lower in calories and can be as satisfying as a meat-and-potatoes meal.

Salt or sodium in the diet is a concern for many. Homemade soups can be prepared without salt or with a very small amount. Herbs can enhance the soup's flavor, preventing a bland, salt-free taste. Broths can be made without salt and used as the base for many other soups. ❧

Soup Terms

The word *soup* probably came from the sound made as one sips or slurps soup from a spoon. Soup is a liquid consisting of a broth with or without pieces of meat, vegetable or fruit. It is the broth that ties all the flavors together in a single dish.

The amount of liquid required for a dish to be called *soup* is open to interpretation. The lines between soups and stews, soups and puddings and soups and porridges are fine and crooked. Usually a soup will slip through the tines of a fork or pour from a spoon. But custom accepts soups as thin as consommé, as thick as a chowder or even almost solid. With Mexican *dry soups* the broth is absorbed by rice, pasta or tortillas as it cooks. There is no liquid left to serve. Soups can be hot or cold. Broth in a gelled soup forms a soft mound in a spoon as it chills.

Because of the variety of foods included under the name of soup, there is considerable confusion. The following definitions may help.

Broth is water flavored by slow simmering with meat, poultry or fish, vegetables and herbs. The broth is strained through cheesecloth to remove all solid material. Fat can be skimmed from the surface. Or the broth may be refrigerated to solidify the fat for easy removal. Broth can be a fine, simple soup on its own, but is usually the base for a variety of soups.

Stock actually refers to food that is on hand. Soup stock is broth made from whatever is available. The terms *stock* and *broth* are often used interchangeably.

Bouillon is the French word for broth. It is also used interchangeably with *broth* and *stock.*

Consommé is a French word referring to a *clarified broth.* After slow simmering, small particles are suspended in broth even after straining. Clarifying removes these small particles, leaving a sparkling, clear broth. If a broth is to be served as a simple soup, it is usually clarified and served as consommé, see Champagne Consommé, page 75. Commercial, canned consommé has gelatin added to give the broth body needed when served alone. Homemade broth has natural gelatin that simmers out of cracked bones. Consommé may be served hot or cold. When chilled, consommé mounds softly on a spoon.

Cream soup does not refer to a soup rich with cream. Though the soup may contain cream, it is not the essential ingredient. A cooked, solid food such as chicken, mushrooms or celery is pureed with a broth or milk. The smooth soup is usually thickened with flour and sometimes egg. Cream soup has a uniform, blended flavor. Small amounts of meat or vegetable pieces may be added as a garnish or to give interest to the soup.

Chowder is named for the pot—*chaudière*—originally used for making it. Thick soups of clam or other seafood or corn cooked in a chaudière, became known as *chowders.* These hearty soups usually have milk, fish broth or chicken broth as the base. Potatoes and salt pork or bacon are almost always included. Clam chowders exemplify the range of diversity in chowders. New England-style is rich and creamy with milk or cream, while Manhattan-style has a clear, tomato-flavored broth. Though chowders may feature various ingredients and look quite different, tradition dictates that chowder be a hearty meal-in-a-bowl.

Bisque is a soup as exquisitely rich and creamy as its French name implies. The richness comes from the thickened sauce of cream and egg used as a base. A hint of sherry or brandy is often added to complement the lobster, scallop or other seafood starring in the soup. Though originally a seafood soup, it may feature other meats or even vegetables. A bisque may be served hot or chilled. Either way, servings should be small. Bisques are rich and meant to tempt and tease the palate, not dull it.

Preparing & Storing Soup

Prepared in a slow cooker, pressure cooker or on the stove top, soups are an easy supper. Making them doesn't require complicated techniques or know-how. Most soups need only a hot bread or simple sandwich and light dessert served with them. Prepare them often for nourishing and satisfying meals.

One of the benefits of preparing a big pot of soup is the leftovers. Most soup-lovers say the flavor is better the second day. This is especially true of soups that are simmered 30 minutes or less. To store soup, cool it quickly. Pour the soup into an airtight container immediately. Plastic storage containers or large jars work well. Immediately put glass jars in the refrigerator. Plastic containers of soup may be cooled in two to three inches of cold water before being put in the refrigerator.

To reheat soup, remove the amount you plan to use. Leave the remainder in the refrigerator. Plan to serve the leftover soup for a quick lunch, a warming afternoon snack or a hurried supper. But use it within two or three days. For longer storage, freeze it.

Soups on hand in the freezer take the worry out of emergency meals. But not all soups freeze well. Chowders, thickened cream soups and soups with milk, eggs or cheese do not freeze well. Potatoes in soup soften during freezing and fall apart when reheated. Bean soups and soups of meat and vegetables in broth are best for freezing. Put the soup in plastic freezer containers or quart jars. Be sure to leave about 1-1/2 inches at the top of the container or jar for expansion. Chill the soup in the refrigerator overnight before freezing. Label the container with the soup name and date. Use it within three months.

Thaw frozen soup overnight in the refrigerator or in a microwave oven on DEFROST or the lowest setting for 15 to 20 minutes. When there hasn't been time to plan ahead, soup can be thawed in two to three inches of cool water. DO NOT put glass jars of frozen soup in *hot* water. When the soup has thawed enough that it can be removed from the container, put it in a saucepan. Cover and heat the soup over low heat, stirring frequently until it is completely thawed. Increase the heat and simmer until ready to serve.

Using a Slow Cooker

Soup can simmer conveniently on a back burner or be prepared quickly on the front of the stove top. Recipe directions throughout the book rely on stove-top cooking of soups. However, a slow cooker can save time and energy in preparing some soups. Simmering bones and meat for broth is especially suited to the slow cooker. The broth must simmer slowly for four or more hours. With a slow cooker, the simmer can be maintained with minimal energy use. When making broth, a slow cooker must have at least a six-quart capacity. If the bones are covered, some of the water can be added later.

Some soups are convenient and satisfying prepared in a slow cooker. Others are not. Broth-type soups can be left simmering in the cooker. The mouth-watering aroma of the soup will greet you as you enter the kitchen. Rich soups that require making a thickened cream sauce of milk or cream and eggs are better prepared on the stove top.

When using a slow cooker, some modification of recipes is necessary. Combine ingredients as the recipe directs, omitting rice, pasta, thickeners like flour or cornstarch, and such dairy products as milk, yogurt, sour cream or cheese. Simmer the soup on LOW for six to eight hours or on HIGH for three to four hours. Add rice or pasta, if called for, 30 minutes before serving. Cook the soup on HIGH until the rice or pasta is tender.

Thicken the soup 10 minutes before serving. Combine the flour or cornstarch with two times as much cold water. For example, if you are using 1/4 cup flour, mix it with 1/2 cup cold water. Stir vigorously until smooth. Slowly pour mixture into hot soup, stirring constantly. Cook soup on HIGH, stirring constantly, until it boils.

Milk, yogurt, sour cream or cheese should be added during final minutes of cooking. Warm the milk before pouring it into hot soup because it may curdle. Gradually stir about 1 cup hot soup into yogurt or sour cream. Then, pour mixture into remaining soup. Heat soup on LOW. Do not allow soup to boil once yogurt or sour cream has been added. Stir grated cheese into soup. Serve when the cheese has melted.

For more information on using a slow cooker for making soup, see *Crockery Cookery* by Mable Hoffman, published by HPBooks.

Using a Pressure Cooker

A pressure cooker can save time in preparing soups. Most soups can be cooked in one-third the time required for ordinary stove-top cooking. The high temperature reached in a pressure cooker quickly extracts the essence of meats and vegetables, creating wonderfully flavored broths.

As with the slow cooker, some soups are better suited to pressure-cooker preparation than others. Chunky meat and vegetable soups that usually require long simmering times cook in 30 to 45 minutes under pressure. Vegetables and broth cooked in a pressure cooker then pureed in a blender or food processor make excellent cream soups. Dried bean, lentil and pea soups can be prepared without the usual planning ahead and still have an incomparably rich heartiness.

When using a pressure cooker some modifications must be made in the recipe. Combine *only* the meat, herbs, spices and vegetables used for seasonings and the liquid, except milk. Do not prepare milk-base soups in a pressure cooker. The cooker must not be more than two-thirds full so you may have to omit some of the liquid called for. Add the extra liquid after cooking. Close the cooker and bring it up to pressure following the manufacturer's directions. Cook the length of time suggested by the manufacturer for the specific meat used. Remove the cooker from the heat and reduce the pressure as instructed by the manufacturer.

At this point, add the remaining ingredients according to the recipe directions. Simmer the soup on the stove top with the lid ajar until these added ingredients are heated through or cooked tender.

Consult the user's manual of your cooker for directions on making vegetable cream soups. *Bean Cookery* by Sue & Bill Deeming, published by HPBooks, gives information on cooking dried beans in a pressure cooker and making bean soups.

The Sandwich Story

Sandwiches probably go back in history as far as the invention of bread. Bread was used to soak up the last traces of food and gravy on the plate. For those who didn't have plates, hunks of bread were used to hold the meat, cheese or stew of the meal. Later, bread was used for pushing food onto the fork.

The earliest written record of a sandwich describes a feast ritual of the Jewish Passover. Rabbi Hillel, a Jewish teacher in the time of Herod, created the custom of eating a mixture of bitter herbs, nuts and apples between two slices of unleavened bread. The unleavened bread, or *matzo*, is like that used by the Jews when they fled from Egypt. In their haste to leave, they had no time to let their bread rise and therefore ate unleavened bread. The bitter filling was to remind the Jews of their suffering in Egypt.

The sandwich didn't receive its name until the Middle Ages. The English Earl of Sandwich ordered two slices of bread to surround roast meat so he could eat and still play cards with greaseless hands. His concoction with all its variations still carries his name.

Sandwiches have always been popular food, often eaten for convenience. Farmers in the field could stop for a lunch of meat, cheese and bread eaten as a sandwich without losing much time. The Indians of Mexico made a flat bread called a *tortilla* which they filled with meat, beans and vegetables. These were rolled or folded for easy eating out of hand. Pita bread or pocket bread is very popular now, but the Arab world has been using it for centuries. The pocket is stuffed with a savory meat mixture, making a sandwich easy to eat with no mess.

Sandwiches are as popular today as ever. They generally suggest an informality that everybody loves. Whether eating it requires knife and fork or plenty of napkins, a sandwich is enjoyed by family and guests of all ages.

Best known as lunch fare or a snack food, sandwiches can be served any time of day. They offer a fun-to-eat change of pace from the regular cereal-and-toast breakfast. Hot and hearty meat sandwiches can satisfy even big supper appetites.

Sandwich possibilities are almost endless because of the variety of breads, spreads and fillings available. Bakeries offer chewy-textured French breads, nutty whole-grain breads, soft white breads and moist dark rye breads. Special bakeries make ethnic breads like bagels, crumpets and pita bread. For the adventurous cook, these breads, with many variations, can be made at home. Fillings of meat, cheese, fish and vegetables can fit any need from low-calorie meals and easy suppers to taste-tempting appetizers. Spreads, like salad dressings, add a zesty flavor that enhances the filling and ties the taste experience together.

Peanut-butter-and-jelly or hamburger sandwiches are in every cook's file of foods to prepare. These and many other sandwiches don't require recipes, only your imagination. The sandwich recipes offered here are meant to spark your interest and give you some new ideas.

Sandwich-Making Tips

Sandwiches are easy to make. In fact, they are often the first food young cooks struggle with when they can barely hold a knife. Here are some tips to help ensure that sandwiches will be fresh-tasting and attractive, not soggy or dried out.

BREAD

Bread used for a sandwich is very important. Good sandwiches can be made from whatever bread is available. But the best taste comes when bread is chosen to complement the filling. When the filling is full-flavored such as the corned beef, Swiss cheese and sauerkraut of a Reuben sandwich, choose a bread with distinctive flavor like rye. When a filling is soft, such as egg salad, a nutty, crunchy whole-wheat bread is ideal.

Whatever bread is used, be sure it is fresh. If a loaf of bread, either store-bought or homemade, will not be used within three days, freeze part of it. After three days, bread begins to dry out, losing its soft texture and fresh taste. Homemade bread can be too fresh for sandwiches. Bread still warm from the oven is heavenly to pop in your mouth, but it does not make good sandwiches. It is difficult to slice and is so tender it tears easily. Allow bread to cool completely before making sandwiches.

SPREADS

Sandwich spreads can be as simple as butter or mayonnaise or as different as Chili-Avocado Spread. They add moistness to sandwiches, complement the flavors of both the bread and filling and sometimes protect the bread from a moist filling.

Spreads, such as seasoned butters and cheese spreads, should be left at room temperature at least 15 minutes to soften. Cold spreads will tear the bread and will not spread evenly. Spreads of all kinds should cover the bread to the edges. When a moist salad mixture is the sandwich filling, such as tuna salad with salad dressing or mayonnaise, a spread is not needed.

FILLINGS

Fillings for sandwiches can be anything from bologna and cheese slices to slivers of chicken in a creamy cheese sauce. Each has its place. Be generous with sandwich fillings. Allow at least two ounces of meat and cheese or 1/2 cup of salad filling for each sandwich. Use smaller amounts for light appetites and waist-watchers.

Fillings can be made up in advance and stored in the refrigerator. They'll be ready for making brown-bag lunches in the morning or for after-school snacks. Use salad mixtures containing eggs, meat or fish within two days.

Sandwiches for packed lunches or picnics should be made without lettuce, tomato slices, sprouts or pickles. These items will lose crispness and can make a sandwich soggy. Wrap them separately to tuck in the sandwich just before eating. They'll add a delightful crunchiness.

Hot fillings quickly soak into bread. Toast the bread first, and serve hot sandwiches immediately.

FREEZING

Freezing sandwiches for packed lunches can save time. If you make a lot of sandwiches every week, you can do them all at once. Wrap them individually in plastic wrap and then in foil, or put in small freezer bags. Take the sandwiches from the freezer and pack them, still frozen, in lunch boxes. By lunchtime, they'll be thawed and remarkably fresh-tasting. Meat sandwiches, like chicken, ham, fish and cold cuts, freeze well. Peanut butter does too. Do not use mayonnaise or salad dressing in sandwiches to be frozen. Substitute sour cream, cream cheese, butter or margarine as the spread or part of the filling. Yolks of hard-cooked eggs freeze well, but whites toughen. If a hard-cooked egg is finely chopped or forced through a sieve, freezing results are acceptable. Natural cheese becomes crumbly when frozen, but processed cheese freezes well. Do not freeze lettuce, tomato, sprouts or other raw vegetables in sandwiches. Add these after sandwiches have thawed.

HEATING

Microwave ovens can make sandwiches hot in less than one minute with no mess. You can warm a complete sandwich or heat just the filling. Full-bodied breads warm better in a microwave oven than soft, white breads.

The most common problem with microwaving complete sandwiches is overheating. Cook on full power (HIGH) only until bread is warm, not hot, and cheese melts or the filling is warm. Meats should be sliced thinly to heat quickly. Bread tends to become soggy then tough. To prevent this, put a paper napkin or plate under the sandwich. A piece of foil, the size of the sandwich, placed in the microwave under the plate or napkin will also protect the bread from overcooking. Whole warmed sandwiches turn out best if the bread is toasted first. Frozen bread slices can also be used. Heat the same length of time as a sandwich made from thawed bread. This process works especially well with hot dogs and frozen buns. Do not microwave frozen sandwiches. The filling will not thaw and warm before the bread becomes tough.

Sandwich fillings may be heated separately and then made into a sandwich. Lay thin slices of meat on a platter or put filling in a microwave-safe dish. Cook on full power (HIGH) 45 seconds to one minute for one sandwich. Assemble the sandwich with warm filling and serve immediately.

To warm sandwiches in an oven, preheat the oven to 350F (175C). Wrap sandwiches individually in foil. Heat until just warm, 10 to 15 minutes.

- If crusts left on plates are a problem at your house, trim the crust before serving. Use the crust to make seasoned crumbs for topping soups or casseroles. Children are especially enchanted with sandwiches cut in animal, people or flower shapes with cookie cutters. Cut the bread first. Then spread generously with filling. Bread scraps can be used for crumbs. Sandwiches cut in shapes also make attractive party plates.
- Sandwiches for parties can be made two hours in advance. Arrange sandwiches on a platter; cover with a clean, damp cloth. Refrigerate until ready to serve.
- Sandwich recipes in this book make four to six servings. For many recipes, you can make one sandwich by using one or two slices of bread and a portion of the meat or cheese and spread. For sandwiches with salad or cooked fillings, the extra filling can be stored in the refrigerator.

Sue & Bill Deeming

Sue Deeming holds a bachelor's degree in Food Science from Iowa State University and a doctorate in Biochemistry and Nutrition from the University of Arizona. Since receiving her degrees, she has worked continually to broaden her food skills. She feels that food quality and nutrition depend greatly on how the food is prepared and served at home. Through books and other projects, Sue shares the results of her food research by providing today's cook with recipes that are flavorful and fun to prepare.

Sue and her husband, Bill, are the authors of two other HPBooks, *Bean Cookery* and *Canning.* They are founders of The Authors' Kitchen, located in Portland, Oregon. This company provides educational and promotional materials on food, recipe development and nutritional consultation for businesses interested in promoting good health. What began as the Deemings' shared interest in food for their own entertainment has grown into the shared excitement of a prospering family business.

Soup Beginnings

Soups from delicate Champagne Consommé to hearty Louisiana Creole Gumbo begin with good broth. Because the broth carries the flavor of the soup, a finished soup will be no better than the broth used to make it. Slowly simmering a mixture of meat, bones, vegetables, herbs and water releases and blends flavors and produces the finest broth. But when time does not allow, highly acceptable broth can be made in 30 minutes starting with commercially canned broth. Whether simmered for hours or prepared in minutes, the object is to produce a liquid brimming with flavor that can be used to create a diversity of soups.

Broths are usually made from beef, beef and veal, chicken, a combination of beef and chicken, or fish. With flavor in mind, use fresh ingredients. Don't make broth by cleaning the refrigerator of leftovers. Ingredients for slow-simmered broth include meat, bones, vegetables, seasonings and water. Both fresh meat or fish and bones are used for flavor. For soup bones, choose meaty neck bones, marrow bones or shin bones. Avoid large joint bones. Large bones should be cracked or cut into 2-inch pieces so flavor and gelatinous material will cook out, giving richness and body to the broth. Vegetables are sliced or chopped to release more of their flavor during cooking. A light seasoning with herbs enhances the meat and vegetable flavors without competing or overpowering. Water covers the ingredients and permits the mingling of flavors during slow simmering.

Quick broths start with a convenient canned broth. Wine, vegetables and herbs are simmered with the broth to give it a fuller, fresher taste. Quick broths can be used in any recipe calling for broth.

Slow-simmered broth is simple to prepare and does not require constant attention. Cooking can be interrupted and continued when it is more convenient. To begin, the meat, bones and vegetables are baked with a little vegetable oil for 30 minutes. This intensifies the meat and vegetable flavors. These ingredients are combined in a stockpot or deep kettle with water to cover. The mixture is brought to a gentle boil. The surface is skimmed to remove foam that could cloud the broth. Herbs and seasonings are added.

The broth should simmer so occasional bubbles come to the surface. Do not allow it to boil vigorously. Heat should be checked to maintain slow simmer. Set the lid ajar. The broth should be looked at occasionally during cooking to be sure ingredients are covered with water. If necessary, hot water should be added.

When the broth is ready, meat and bones are removed. Meat may be used in a stew or casserole or added back in making the soup. Bones are discarded. The broth is strained into a large bowl through a sieve lined with cheesecloth. Vegetables and herbs are discarded. The finished broth should be tasted. If desired, broth can be boiled, uncovered, over medium-high heat so the liquid is reduced, intensifying flavor.

If the hot broth is to be used immediately to make soup, strain the broth and set it aside to cool 15 to 20 minutes. Fat droplets will come together, forming a layer on top that can be skimmed off with a spoon. To get rid of the last traces of fat, pull strips of paper towel across the surface to soak up fat. Broth is then ready to use.

If the broth is not to be used immediately, it should be cooled, uncovered, in the refrigerator until a fat layer rises to the top and solidifies. Remove and discard this fat layer. Usually the broth will gel as it cools.

It should be spooned into jars or plastic containers for storage. Beef, meat or chicken broth can be stored in the refrigerator two to three days. For storage up to four months, it should be frozen. Fish broth can be kept up to 24 hours in the refrigerator or two months in the freezer. Remember to leave 1-1/2 inches of space at the top of the jars or containers for expansion during freezing.

Included with broths in this chapter is a basic soup recipe and two dry mixes.

Cream-of-Any-Vegetable Soup is a recipe you will use again and again. Use it to make fresh broccoli soup in January and fresh zucchini soup in August. Or, use frozen vegetables year round.

Country-Vegetable-Soup Mix is a time and space saver for meals on the road. Whether camping, backpacking or traveling in an R.V., a hot meal of soup can be a snap. Five-Bean-Soup Mix is perfect for easy meals at home. Store it, tightly covered, on your pantry shelf and fresh, homemade soup will be a supper you won't have to plan ahead. ☙

Meat Broth

This mild-flavored broth can be substituted for beef broth in any recipe.

2 tablespoons vegetable oil
2 whole cloves
2 medium onions, cut in quarters
1 carrot, sliced
1 celery stalk including leafy top, sliced
4 lbs. meaty beef and veal bones,
　　cracked in 2-inch pieces
1 lb. chicken wings, backs, necks

3 qts. water
2 garlic cloves
1 bay leaf
1/4 teaspoon dried leaf thyme
1/4 teaspoon dried leaf marjoram
4 parsley sprigs
2 teaspoons salt

Preheat oven to 450F (230C). Pour 1 tablespoon vegetable oil in a 13'' x 9'' baking pan. Insert a whole clove in 2 of the onion quarters. Add onions, carrot and celery to pan; toss vegetables to coat with oil. Add bones and chicken pieces. Sprinkle remaining 1 tablespoon oil over bones. Bake until all pieces are well browned, about 30 minutes, turning pieces several times during baking. Put bones and vegetables in a 6- or 8-quart pot. Add about 1 cup water to baking pan. Stir up browned bits in pan so they dissolve in water; add to pot. Add remaining water to pot. Use more water, if necessary, to cover all ingredients. Slowly bring mixture to a simmer. Do not boil. Skim foam from surface until surface is clear. Flatten garlic cloves with the side of a knife. Add flattened garlic, bay leaf, thyme, marjoram, parsley and salt to broth. Slowly simmer broth, with lid ajar, 5 to 6 hours. Remove bones and vegetables with a slotted spoon; discard. Line a sieve with cheesecloth. Strain broth through sieve into a glass container. Discard solid ingredients. To use immediately, spoon liquid fat from surface of hot broth. To use later, cool broth at room temperature 30 minutes. Refrigerate until fat layer solidifies on top. Remove and discard fat. Refrigerate, tightly covered, up to 3 days. For longer storage, freeze in an airtight container, leaving 1-1/2 inches headspace. Makes about 2 quarts.

Beef Broth

Do not use knuckle or joint bones unless they are meaty and cut in pieces.

2 tablespoons vegetable oil
1 medium onion, cut in quarters
1 carrot, sliced
1 celery stalk
2 lbs. meaty beef and veal bones,
   including at least 1 lb. marrow bones,
   cracked in 2-inch pieces
2 lbs. beef shank meat or other lean meat,
   cut in 1-inch cubes

3 qts. water
1 bay leaf
6 parsley sprigs
1/4 teaspoon dried leaf basil
2 teaspoons salt
2 garlic cloves, minced
1 medium tomato, cored, cut in quarters
1/2 cup fresh mushroom pieces

Preheat oven to 450F (230C). Pour 1 tablespoon vegetable oil in a 13" x 9" baking pan. Add onion, carrot and celery to pan; toss vegetables to coat with oil. Add bones and meat cubes. Sprinkle remaining 1 tablespoon oil over bones. Bake until all pieces are well browned, about 30 minutes, turning pieces several times during baking. Place bones, meat cubes and vegetables in a 6- or 8-quart pot. Add about 1 cup water to baking pan. Stir up browned bits in pan so they dissolve in water; add to pot. Add remaining water to pot. Use more water, if necessary, to cover all ingredients. Slowly bring mixture to simmer. Do not boil. Skim foam from surface until surface is clear. Add remaining ingredients. Slowly simmer broth, with lid ajar, 5 to 6 hours. Remove bones, meat and vegetables with a slotted spoon. Meat may be set aside to add back to the final soup. Discard bones and vegetables. Line a sieve with cheesecloth. Strain broth through sieve into a glass container. Discard solid ingredients. To use immediately, spoon liquid fat from surface of hot broth. To use later, cool broth at room temperature 30 minutes. Refrigerate until fat layer solidifies on top. Remove and discard fat. Refrigerate, tightly covered, up to 3 days. For longer storage, freeze in an airtight container, leaving 1-1/2 inches headspace. Makes about 2 quarts.

Quick Beef Broth

If using concentrated beef broth in 10-1/2-ounce cans, dilute first with water.

1 teaspoon vegetable oil
1/4 chopped onion
1/4 cup sliced carrot
1 tablespoon chopped celery
2 (14-1/2-oz.) cans regular-strength beef
   broth, or 2 (10-1/2-oz.) cans
   concentrated beef broth and
   1-1/2 cups water

1/3 cup dry red wine, if desired
1 bay leaf
1/8 teaspoon dried leaf basil
Salt and pepper to taste

In a medium saucepan, heat oil. Add onion, carrot and celery; sauté until onion is tender. Add beef broth, water, if required, and wine, if desired. Stir in bay leaf and basil. Bring broth to a boil; reduce heat. Cover and simmer 20 minutes. Line a sieve with cheesecloth. Strain broth through sieve into a glass container. Discard vegetables and herbs. Season to taste with salt and pepper. Use broth immediately or refrigerate, tightly covered, up to 3 days. Makes about 3-1/2 cups.

How to Make Beef Broth

1/Bake meat bones and vegetables until well browned, turning several times during baking.

2/Slowly bring mixture to a simmer. Skim foam from surface until surface is clear.

Cream-of-Any-Vegetable Soup

A quick soup with so many possibilities it's never boring.

**3 cups chopped fresh or frozen vegetable,
    such as zucchini, broccoli,
    spinach or celery
1 cup Chicken Broth, page 16, or
    regular-strength canned chicken broth
3 tablespoons butter or margarine**

**1/4 cup all-purpose flour
1 cup milk
1 egg, beaten
1 cup half and half
Salt and white pepper to taste**

Put chopped vegetable and broth in a 3-quart saucepan. Bring to a boil; reduce heat. Cover pan and simmer until vegetable is tender, 15 to 20 minutes. Puree vegetable and liquid in a blender or food processor. Melt butter or margarine in the saucepan. Add flour; stir until smooth. Gradually stir in milk. Bring to a boil, stirring constantly. Add vegetable puree. In a small bowl, combine egg and half and half. Gradually pour egg mixture into milk mixture, stirring constantly. Cook over medium-low heat, stirring frequently, until heated through, about 5 minutes. Do not boil. Season to taste with salt and white pepper. Makes 6 (1-cup) servings.

Chicken Broth

Broth will gel when cooled. Simply spoon out or pour into pot like liquid broth.

2 lbs. chicken backs, necks, wings
2 qts. water
1 medium onion, cut in quarters
1 celery stalk including leafy top, sliced
1 medium carrot, sliced
2 teaspoons salt

1 bay leaf
1/2 teaspoon dried leaf thyme
1/2 teaspoon dried leaf basil
1 teaspoon dried leaf parsley
10 black peppercorns

Place chicken backs, necks and wings in a 6-quart pot; add water. Bring to a simmer. Skim foam from surface until surface is clear. Reduce heat to maintain a gentle simmer. Add remaining ingredients. Simmer, with lid ajar, 3 hours. Line a sieve with cheesecloth. Strain broth through sieve into a glass container. Discard bones, vegetables and herbs. To use immediately, spoon liquid fat from surface of hot broth. To use later, cool broth at room temperature. Refrigerate until a fat layer solidifes on top. Remove and discard fat layer. Refrigerate, tightly covered, up to 3 days. For longer storage, freeze in an airtight container, leaving 1-1/2 inches headspace. Makes about 6 cups.

Variation

Ginger-Chicken Broth: Add 2 (1/4-inch) slices fresh gingerroot, peeled, with vegetables. Simmer and strain as above.

Pressure-Cooker Chicken Broth

Flavorful homemade broth cooks in only 30 minutes.

1-1/2 lbs. chicken pieces
1 qt. water
2 chicken bouillon cubes
1 small onion, sliced
1 celery stalk, sliced

1 carrot, sliced
1 bay leaf
1/4 teaspoon dried leaf thyme
6 black peppercorns
1 teaspoon salt

Place chicken on a rack in a 4-quart or larger pressure cooker. Be sure cooker is no more than 2/3 full. Add remaining ingredients. Check vent in cooker lid. Clear vent, if necessary. Place lid on cooker. Bring cooker up to 15-pounds pressure, following manufacturer's directions. Maintain pressure 30 minutes. Remove cooker from heat. Cool cooker by running warm water over lid. Open cooker carefully, following manufacturer's directions. Remove chicken pieces. Use for chicken fricassee, crepes or salad. Line a sieve with cheesecloth. Strain broth through sieve into a glass container. Discard vegetables and herbs. To use immediately, spoon liquid fat from surface of hot broth. To use later, cool broth at room temperature 30 minutes. Refrigerate until fat layer solidifies on top. Remove and discard fat. Refrigerate, tightly covered, up to 3 days. For longer storage, freeze in an airtight container, leaving 1-1/2 inches headspace. Makes about 1 quart.

How to Make Chicken Broth

1/Strain broth into a glass container. To use in soup immediately, spoon liquid fat from surface of hot broth.

2/To use later, cool broth at room temperature. Refrigerate until fat solidifies on top. Remove and discard fat.

Quick Chicken Broth

Start with canned broth and season to freshen and enhance the flavor.

2 teaspoons vegetable oil
1/4 cup chopped onion
1/4 cup sliced carrot
1/4 cup chopped celery
2 (14-1/2-oz.) cans regular-strength
   chicken broth

1/3 cup dry white wine, if desired
1/2 bay leaf
1/8 teaspoon dried leaf thyme
Salt and white pepper to taste

In a medium saucepan, heat oil. Add onion, carrot and celery; sauté until onion is tender. Add broth and wine, if desired. Stir in bay leaf and thyme. Bring to a boil; reduce heat. Cover pan and simmer 20 minutes. Line a sieve with cheesecloth. Strain broth through sieve into a glass container. Discard vegetables and herbs. Season to taste with salt and white pepper. Use broth immediately or refrigerate, tightly covered, up to 3 days. Makes about 3-1/2 cups.

Country-Vegetable-Soup Mix

Dried vegetable flakes can be found in supermarket spice sections.

1 cup dried lentils
1 cup dried yellow split peas
1 cup dried green split peas
4 (.87-oz.) cans dried mixed vegetable
    flakes (2 cups)
2 tablespoons granulated chicken or
    beef bouillon

1 cup uncooked pearl barley or brown rice
1/2 cup dried minced onion
1/2 teaspoon salt
1 tablespoon dried leaf parsley
2 teaspoons dried leaf basil

Sort lentils and split peas. In a large mixing bowl or airtight container, combine all ingredients. Stir to distribute ingredients evenly. Store in a plastic bag or tightly closed container at room temperature. Always stir soup base before measuring and using. Makes about 6 cups soup mix or enough for 32 cups soup.

To Make: Country-Vegetable Soup
Combine 1-1/2 cups soup mix and 1 quart water in a 3-quart saucepan. Bring to a boil; cover and simmer over low heat until peas and lentils are tender, 45 to 60 minutes. Stir in 2 to 3 cups vegetable-juice cocktail or tomato juice until soup is desired thickness. Season to taste with salt and pepper. Makes 4 (2-cup) servings.

Five-Bean-Soup Mix

An easy soup that can be stored ready-mixed on the shelf.

1-1/2 cups dried pinto beans
1 cup dried large lima beans
1-1/2 cups dried navy beans or
    small white beans
1 cup dried kidney beans
1 cup dried garbanzo beans
1/2 cup dried minced onion

1 tablespoon granulated beef bouillon
1 tablespoon granulated chicken bouillon
2 teaspoons salt
1/2 teaspoon garlic salt
1 tablespoon paprika
1/4 cup bacon bits
1 teaspoon dry mustard

Sort dried beans; place in a large airtight container. In a small bowl, combine onion, beef and chicken bouillon, salt, garlic salt, paprika, bacon bits and mustard. Stir with a fork to distribute all ingredients evenly. Pour seasonings into a plastic bag. Tie bag tightly. Place bag in bean container. Store, tightly covered, at room temperature. Makes about 7 cups soup mix or enough for 30 cups soup.

To Make: Five-Bean Soup
Place 1-1/2 cups bean mixture in a sieve. Rinse under running water. Place beans in a 3-quart saucepan; add 5 cups water and 1 tablespoon vegetable oil. Add 1/4 cup seasoning mix. Bring to a boil; reduce heat. Cover and simmer until beans are tender, 2 to 2-1/2 hours. Stir in 1 (8-ounce) can tomato sauce. Simmer 10 minutes longer. Makes 4 (1-1/2-cup) servings.

Ingredients for Homemade Broth

Fish Broth

If fish heads and bones are difficult to find, use inexpensive fish fillets.

3 lbs. fish heads and bones or
   2 lbs. lean fresh fish
1 medium onion, sliced
1 medium carrot, sliced
1 celery stalk including leafy top, sliced
2 teaspoons lemon juice

1 cup dry white wine
6 cups water
1 bay leaf
1 teaspoon salt
1/4 teaspoon dried leaf tarragon

Wash fish heads and bones under running cold water; discard any skin. Put heads and bones or lean fish in a 4-quart pot. Add onion, carrot, celery, lemon juice, wine and water. Add more water, if necessary, to cover ingredients. Bring to a simmer; do not boil. Reduce heat to maintain simmer. Skim foam from surface until surface is clear. Stir in bay leaf, salt and tarragon. Partially cover and simmer 30 minutes. Line a sieve with cheesecloth. Strain broth through sieve into a glass container. Discard bones and vegetables. Use broth immediately in fish soups or chowders or store, tightly covered, in refrigerator up to 24 hours. For longer storage, freeze in an airtight container, leaving 1-1/2 inches headspace. Makes about 6 cups.

Quick Fish Broth

Clam juice is readily available in supermarkets. Look for it near canned fish.

1 tablespoon vegetable oil
1 medium onion, sliced
1/4 cup chopped celery
1/4 cup sliced fresh mushrooms
2 cups bottled clam juice

1 cup water
1 cup dry white wine
1/8 teaspoon dried leaf thyme
1 small bay leaf

Heat oil in a 3-quart saucepan over medium-high heat. Add onion, celery and mushrooms; sauté until mushrooms darken and onion is tender. Add clam juice, water, wine, thyme and bay leaf. Bring to a simmer; reduce heat and simmer, uncovered, 30 minutes. Line a sieve with cheesecloth. Strain broth through sieve into a glass container. Discard vegetables and herbs. Use broth immediately in fish soups and chowders or refrigerate, tightly covered, up to 24 hours. Makes about 1 quart.

If a soup is too salty, add a peeled potato. Simmer 15 minutes, then remove the potato. Potato will take up some of the salty taste.

Soup Toppers

Crumbling crackers into tomato soup, to many mothers' dismay, is a child's way of adding fun to soup. A variety of soup toppers can do the same thing in a more acceptable way. Soup toppers dress up a simple soup making it something special. They also make a soup more interesting and filling. Basil & Cheese Dumplings simmered in a tomato or vegetable soup make the soup more of a meal.

Almost all soups benefit from a topping, whether a simple sprinkling of cheese or Seasoned Croutons or a more elaborate dumpling or cracker. Add the topper to each bowl as it is served. Or, pass the topper for each individual to add his own. Served either way, soup toppers add contrasting color, texture and sometimes temperature. Toppers can range from Cracker Balls in a colorful chicken-vegetable soup or yellow Corn Cakes in a steaming bowl of chili. Toppers often highlight an ingredient included in the soup. Thin slices of broccoli floating on a bowl of cream-of-broccoli soup add an elegant touch.

Some soup toppers, such as dumplings or Corn Cakes, must be prepared when the soup is made. Others can be made ahead and stored. Cracker Balls, Animal Crackers, Won-Ton Bows and Almond Crunch can be stored in airtight containers, ready to use in many different soups.

Soup toppers should fit the soup, adding color, crunchiness or an enhancing flavor when needed. Lots of simple toppers are readily available on your kitchen shelf. Top soups with chopped nuts or seeds, popcorn, pretzels or crackers. A dollop of sour cream or yogurt is refreshing in a spicy soup. Add thin slices of the fruit or vegetable featured in the soup. Or, choose a fruit or vegetable with a flavor or texture that will complement the soup. Such an addition is especially appropriate on creamed or pureed soups. Crumbled bacon, sliced hard-cooked egg or egg pressed through a sieve are all easy toppers. Fresh chopped herbs like parsley, dill, cilantro or chives may sometimes be just the right touch. ❧

Menu

Ladies' Luncheon

Artichoke Soup, page 72, with
Crab Dumplings, page 27
Artist's Palettes, page 140
Jellied Strawberry-Swirl Soup, page 151

Oriental-Flavor Family Supper

Sherried Mushroom Soup, page 100, with
Won-Ton Knots, page 26
Sweet & Sour Pork
Steamed Rice
Paradise Wedges, page 153

Cheese Pretzels

These are best eaten when fresh; salt makes them soften during storage.

2 cups all-purpose flour
1/4 teaspoon salt
1/4 teaspoon baking soda
1/4 cup shortening
1-1/2 cups shredded Cheddar cheese (6 oz.)

1/3 cup water
1 egg
1/4 cup milk
2 tablespoons coarse salt

Sift together flour, salt and baking soda into a medium bowl. Cut in shortening with a pastry blender or a fork until mixture resembles coarse meal. Add cheese; toss. Add water, 1 tablespoon at a time, while stirring dough. Turn out dough onto a floured surface. Gently knead until dough holds together and is smooth. Preheat oven to 300F (150C). Roll about 1 tablespoon dough into a 6-inch rope. Place rope on ungreased baking sheet, crossing ends 1-1/2 inches from tips. Press dough together. Lift dough loop formed by crossing rope ends over dough ends. Shape dough as needed with your hands to make pretzel shape. Repeat with remaining dough. In a small bowl, beat egg and milk. Brush pretzels with egg mixture. Sprinkle with coarse salt. Bake until pretzels are browned and firm, about 20 minutes. Cool on a rack. Store completely cooled pretzels in an airtight container. Makes about 36.

Spinach Pesto

Similar to the classic pesto made with fresh basil and pine nuts; use to top Minestrone, page 128.

2 cups fresh parsley sprigs
1 cup fresh spinach leaves
1/3 cup vegetable oil
1/3 cup olive oil

2 garlic cloves, minced
1 teaspoon salt
1/2 cup freshly grated Parmesan cheese
   (1-1/2 oz.)

Combine parsley, spinach, vegetable oil, olive oil, garlic and salt in a blender or food processor; process until smooth. Turn into a small bowl. Stir in Parmesan cheese. Makes 1 cup.

Basil & Cheese Dumplings

Dumplings are best simmered in broth-type soups. Try these in a chunky-vegetable soup.

1 tablespoon butter or margarine
1 tablespoon snipped fresh chives or
   sliced green onion
1/2 teaspoon dried leaf basil

1/2 cup creamed cottage cheese (4 oz.)
1 cup sifted all-purpose flour
1/2 teaspoon salt
1 teaspoon baking powder

Melt butter or margarine in a small skillet. Add chives or green onion and basil. Cook, stirring constantly, until herbs soften. Remove skillet from heat. Stir in cottage cheese; set aside. Sift together flour, salt and baking powder into a medium bowl. Add cottage-cheese mixture. Stir until combined. Drop by rounded teaspoonfuls into simmering soup. Cover soup and simmer until dumplings are firm, about 15 minutes. Makes about 12.

How to Make Cheese Pretzels

1/Place 6-inch dough piece on baking sheet, crossing ends 1-1/2 inches from tips. Press dough together.

2/ Lift dough loop formed by crossing rope ends over dough ends. Shape dough as needed with your hands.

Cracker Balls

A fun shape to float in soup or pop in your mouth for a snack.

1 teaspoon distilled white vinegar	**1/2 teaspoon salt**
1/3 cup milk	**1/4 teaspoon baking soda**
1-1/2 cups sifted all-purpose flour	**1/3 cup shortening**

In a small bowl, stir vinegar into milk; set aside 5 minutes. Sift together flour, salt and baking soda into a medium bowl. Cut in shortening with a pastry blender or fork until mixture resembles coarse meal. Add milk to flour mixture. Stir until flour is moistened. Turn out dough onto a floured surface. Knead until dough holds together and is smooth, about 3 minutes. Preheat oven to 300F (150C). Roll 1 teaspoon dough between hands to form a ball. Put ball on an ungreased baking sheet. Repeat with remaining dough. Space balls 1 inch apart. Bake until cracker balls just begin to brown. Remove to a cooling rack. Store completely cooled cracker balls in an airtight container. Makes about 24.

Animal Crackers

Cut small circles, if animal cutters are not available.

1 cup all-purpose flour
1/4 teaspoon salt
1/2 teaspoon baking powder
1/2 cup freshly grated Parmesan cheese
   (1-1/2 oz.)

3 tablespoons butter or margarine
5 to 6 tablespoons water

In a mixing bowl, combine flour, salt, baking powder and cheese. Cut in butter or margarine with a pastry blender or fork until mixture resembles coarse meal. Add water, 1 tablespoon at a time, until dough holds together. Preheat oven to 300F (150C). Roll out dough on a lightly floured surface to 1/8 inch thick. Cut into animal shapes with 2-inch cookie cutters. Put on an ungreased baking sheet. Bake until lightly browned and crisp, 12 to 15 minutes. Remove crackers to a cooling rack. Store completely cooled crackers in an airtight container. Makes about 30.

Seasoned Croutons

Whole-wheat and rye breads make croutons with a nutty, full flavor.

3 tablespoons butter or margarine
1 small garlic clove, minced
1/4 teaspoon seasoned salt
1 teaspoon chopped fresh parsley or
   1/4 teaspoon dried leaf parsley
1/8 teaspoon dried leaf basil

Pinch dried leaf thyme
Pinch dried dillweed
2 tablespoons freshly grated Parmesan cheese
8 slices firm-textured bread
1 tablespoon olive oil

In a small bowl, combine butter or margarine, garlic, seasoned salt, parsley, basil, thyme and dillweed. Cream with the back of a spoon until well mixed. Stir in Parmesan cheese. Spread 1 side of each slice of bread with butter or margarine mixture. Stack bread in 2 piles of 4 slices each. Cut stacks in 1/4-inch-wide strips. Cut each strip in 1/4-inch cubes. Preheat oven to 200F (95C). Heat olive oil in a heavy, ovenproof skillet over medium heat 1 minute. Add bread cubes; stir to separate and coat. Cook, stirring constantly, 3 to 5 minutes. Place skillet in oven. Bake until cubes are dry and crisp, but not browned, about 15 minutes. Cool completely. Store in an airtight container. Makes about 3 cups.

Variations

Chili-Pepper Croutons: Use 8 slices firm-textured white bread. To 2 tablespoons butter or margarine, add 1 minced garlic clove, 1/2 teaspoon chili powder, a pinch of ground cumin and a pinch of red (cayenne) pepper. Omit other seasonings and cheese. Substitute vegetable oil for olive oil. Prepare and bake croutons as directed above.
Onion-Rye Croutons: Use 8 slices rye bread. To 2 tablespoons butter or margarine, add 1 teaspoon grated onion, 1 teaspoon prepared mustard and a pinch of paprika. Omit other seasonings and cheese. Substitute vegetable oil for olive oil. Prepare and bake croutons as directed above.

Mississippi Meatball Burgoo, page 79, and Animal Crackers.

Won-Ton Knots

Great with an oriental-style soup.

**2 tablespoons butter or margarine,
  room temperature**
1/2 teaspoon soy sauce
Pinch paprika

1/4 teaspoon dry mustard
1/4 teaspoon Worcestershire sauce
4 egg-roll wrappers

Preheat oven to 375F (190C). In a small bowl, combine butter or margarine, soy sauce, paprika, mustard and Worcestershire sauce. Blend with the back of a spoon. Spread 1 side of each egg-roll wrapper with seasoned butter or margarine. Cut each in 1/2-inch-wide strips. Tie each strip in a loose knot. Place on an ungreased baking sheet. Bake until lightly browned, about 5 minutes. Remove knots immediately to a cooling rack. Store completely cooled knots in an airtight container. When dropped in soup, these soften like pasta. To keep them crisp, serve separately. Makes about 48.

How to Make Won-Ton Knots

1/Spread 1 side of egg-roll wrapper with seasoned butter or margarine. Cut wrapper in 1/2-inch strips.

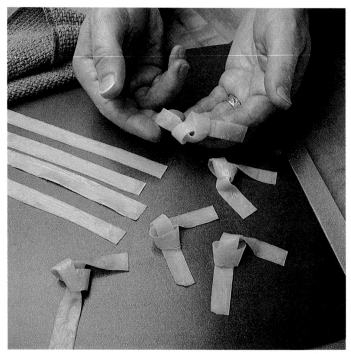

2/Tie each strip of egg-roll wrapper in a loose knot. Place knot on an ungreased baking sheet.

Crab Dumplings

Great addition to vegetable or fish chowders.

1/4 cup butter or margarine,
   room temperature
1/4 cup all-purpose flour
1 teaspoon dry sherry or dry white wine

1 egg yolk
1/3 cup shredded cooked crabmeat
Pinch white pepper

Combine butter or margarine and flour in a small bowl; cream with the back of a spoon until smooth. Stir in sherry and egg yolk. Add crabmeat and white pepper; stir until blended. Dust your hands with flour. Shape rounded teaspoonfuls of dumpling mixture into small balls. To cook, drop dumplings in simmering soup 15 minutes before soup is done. Cover and simmer until dumplings are firm, about 15 minutes. Makes about 18.

Variation

Shrimp, Lobster or Tuna Dumplings: Substitute diced cooked shrimp, shredded cooked lobster or tuna for crabmeat.

Corn Cakes

Float on steaming bowls of Chilly-Day Chili, page 109.

1-1/2 cups water
1/4 teaspoon salt
1/8 teaspoon garlic salt

1/2 cup hominy grits or cornmeal
1/2 cup shredded processed American cheese
   (2 oz.)

Boil water, salt and garlic salt in a saucepan. Slowly add grits or cornmeal, stirring constantly. Cook about 5 minutes, stirring constantly, until mixture is very thick. Add cheese; stir until melted. Drop by rounded teaspoonfuls on an ungreased baking sheet. Cool completely. Spoonfuls of mixture can be stored on baking sheet in refrigerator overnight. Preheat oven to 400F (205C). Using your hands, shape each spoonful of dough into a ball; flatten between palms. Return to baking sheet. Bake 10 minutes. Serve hot from oven. Makes about 18.

Almond Crunch

Serve this crispy oat topping on fruit soups.

1/2 cup sliced almonds
1 cup all-purpose flour
1/2 cup quick-cooking rolled oats

1/4 cup packed brown sugar
1/2 cup butter or margarine

Toast almonds in a heavy skillet over low heat. Stir constantly until lightly browned. Remove almonds immediately. Preheat oven to 400F (205C). Combine flour, oats and brown sugar in a medium bowl. Cut in butter or margarine to form crumbs. Stir in almonds. Pat mixture into an ungreased 8-inch-square baking pan. Bake 15 minutes. Cool in pan 10 minutes. Break up mixture with a metal spoon to make crumbs. Store completely cooled crumbs in an airtight container. Makes about 2 cups.

Breads, Rolls, Spreads & Sauces

Super sandwiches are created when you use a bread or roll with the right flavor and complementing texture. Many breads add their own distinctive characteristics to a sandwich. The nutty chewiness of whole-wheat bread will create a very different peanut-butter sandwich than moist, tender potato bread. Specialty breads, like bagels and crumpets, make out-of-the-ordinary sandwiches that are fun to eat. The delectable sandwich breads and rolls that follow will fit any taste.

Many excellent bakeries produce breads and sandwich rolls in all sizes and shapes. You don't have to bake your own bread to make great sandwiches. Some types of bread are better store-bought. Bread from a French or Italian bakery will have a crisp, chewy, golden crust and soft, sweet interior that is very difficult to duplicate at home. But generally, home-baked bread will be fresher and have a unique taste of its own.

Spreads join together bread or roll and a sandwich filling. Seasoned butters, mayonnaises, cheese spreads and nut butters add subtle flavors that complement both bread and filling. No sandwich is complete without one of them. Imagine a hot dog without mustard!

Spreads in this chapter can be used in a variety of ways. Make your own sandwich creations combining various seasoned butters with cold cuts and cheeses. Add flavored mayonnaises to chicken, tuna or egg salad. Let your imagination go. Some of the spreads also make scrumptious sandwiches on their own. Pepper-Cheese Spread on a toasted slice of English-Muffin Bread or a Crumpet is a tasty breakfast with juice and coffee. Sesame-Nut Butter on thin slices of Squaw Bread makes a deliciously satisfying snack with an apple or pear.

Sandwich-making will be more convenient and creative if you keep a supply of different bread spreads ready at all times.

Bread-making is a satisfying activity. The aroma of a

Menu

Good for Lunch

Country-Vegetable Soup, page 18
Whole-Wheat Bagels, page 41, with
Garden-Vegetable Spread, page 38
Lemonade

After-School Snack

Toasted Cornmeal-English-
Muffin Bread, page 51, with
Pepper-Cheese Spread, page 47
Cranapple Juice

beautiful golden loaf will draw *hmmm's* and *aaah's*. And you may become famous for your Cheddar-Cheese Bread or Poppy-Seed Egg Bread. Some specialty breads, such as Crumpets or Corn-Rye Bagels, may not be available in your area. Recipes for these and many others are included so you can make them yourself.

Most recipes in this chapter are for yeast breads. They are easy to make, but the yeast needs time to grow, making the bread rise. Bread-making is a time-consuming process, but it doesn't require constant attention. A heavy-duty mixer with a bread hook can save time by quickly kneading the dough. But you should never rush the rising process.

When four hours aren't available to concentrate on bread-making, the process can be interrupted. Allow the dough or shaped loaf to rise in the refrigerator while you are gone. It will rise more slowly. When you return, simply remove the dough from the refrigerator and shape into a loaf, if necessary. Let it rise until light, allowing extra time because the dough will be cold. If the refrigerated dough is already shaped into a loaf, let it stand at room temperature 15 minutes. Then put it in a preheated oven. Add 5 minutes to the baking time. Interrupting bread-making in this way is not ideal, but the results are good.

Quick fruit and nut breads use baking powder instead of yeast for rising. They are easy to make and take about half the time required by yeast breads. Quick breads are usually sweet and their use for sandwiches is limited.

Though time-consuming, bread-making is straightforward and uncomplicated. Recipes are easy to follow because they all use similar procedures and differ only in some ingredients. The steps that follow explain the procedure and give tips that will make bread-making most rewarding.

Storing Spreads

Most bread spreads should be stored in the refrigerator. Any containing cheese or mayonnaise **must** be refrigerated. Seasoned butters keep longer and maintain their texture when chilled. Nut butters may be stored at room temperature. After several days, oil will separate and form a layer on the top. This does not mean the nut butter is spoiled. Do not pour off or discard the oil layer. The remaining nut butter would be very dry. Simply stir the oil back into the spread. Storing nut butters in the refrigerator helps prevent this separation.

Some spreads keep better than others. Cheese spreads can be kept in covered containers up to one week in the refrigerator. Most seasoned butters and mayonnaises stay fresh in airtight containers four to six weeks. However, seasoned butters made with unsalted butter keep only one week. Nut butters may be stored several months. Only spreads with fresh chopped fruits or vegetables or fresh herbs must be used quickly. These spreads should be kept only two or three days.

All spreads need time for flavors to blend and develop before being used. Refrigerate spreads eight hours or more before using.

For ease in spreading, allow butters or cheese spreads to soften before using. Nothing is more frustrating than hard butter that tears the bread. Take the spread out of the refrigerator 30 minutes before using.

Steps to Successful Bread-Making

ACTIVATING THE YEAST

Yeast, in either dry or compressed cake form, must be activated to begin growing. Water rehydrates the yeast, but temperature is critical. Warm water—105F (40C)—will encourage quick growth. If the water is too hot—125F (50C) or more—it will kill the yeast. Measure the water temperature with a candy thermometer to be sure the temperature is right. If you do not have a thermometer, run the water over your wrist. If it feels definitely warm, but not hot, the temperature is right. It is always better to have the water a little cooler than needed rather than too hot.

Yeast is dissolved in warm water with added sugar or honey. These sweeteners provide food for the yeast and encourage growth. When the yeast mixture is set aside in a warm place for 15 minutes, it will become foamy. If there are no signs of bubbles, the yeast is not alive. Try a new package of yeast.

MAKING THE DOUGH

Warmth stimulates yeast growth, so all ingredients should be room temperature or warmer. Warm the liquid used in the bread. Milk should be scalded, then cooled to warm. Heating causes certain protein factors in milk to settle out as a residue in the bottom of the pan. When milk is scalded, bread has a finer texture and greater volume.

Making bread dough involves two steps. First, combine the foamy yeast mixture, warm liquid, oil or melted butter or margarine, salt, seasonings and part of the flour. The result is a dough called the *sponge*. This sponge dough is beaten until smooth, then set aside in a warm place for 20 minutes. This initial step starts the yeast and makes the finished dough rise more quickly.

The remaining flour is added, 1/2 cup at a time, until dough is difficult to beat by hand and pulls away from the sides of the bowl. The amount of flour necessary varies depending on current weather conditions and the type of flour used. If too much flour is added, dough will be stiff and hard to knead. The finished bread will be dry and heavy. If not enough flour is added, dough will be sticky. The bread will be too moist, soft and coarse in texture.

The number of different flours available can make bread-making a constantly changing experience. Part of the flour must be made from wheat to give the dough elasticity. This makes the bread rise and keep its shape when baked. Wheat flour may be whole-wheat flour, bleached or unbleached all-purpose flour or bread flour.

Bread flour is made from hard wheat and has a higher protein content than all-purpose flour. Many recipes in this chapter use bread flour in combination with other flours. The resulting bread has a softer texture and is more moist than bread made completely with all-purpose flour. However, all-purpose flour can be used in place of bread flour.

Cornmeal is added to some breads to give a coarse, crunchy texture and distinctly different taste.

Gluten flour is made from wheat but has more wheat protein or *gluten* added to it. This flour is used in French- and Italian-style breads and gives them their characteristic chewiness.

Rye flour alone will not create an elastic dough and high light bread. But when combined with wheat flour, the resulting bread has a firm texture and full hearty flavor.

Flour does not have to be sifted. Spoon it into a measuring cup and level it with a straight knife or handle. Do not pack or tap the flour in the cup.

KNEADING

Kneading the dough develops the protein structure essential to the rising of bread. A heavy-duty mixer with a bread hook makes quick work of this process. But hand kneading is not a vigorous, tiring exercise. Many people find the gentle, rhythmic repetition soothing in a busy day.

To knead dough, lightly sprinkle a clean work surface or board with flour. Place dough in center. Lightly sprinkle additional flour on the dough. Lift the side of dough opposite you and pull it toward you until it is folded almost in half.

Push down and away from you at the folded edge, using the heels of your hands. Turn dough a quarter of a turn or 90 degrees, and repeat. Add flour, as necessary, to keep dough from sticking. Be careful not to add too much flour or dough will become stiff and dry.

As you knead, dough will become springy, smooth and elastic. Its surface will no longer be rough and pebbly. This may take 10 to 15 minutes by hand or about five minutes using a mixer. It is impossible to knead too much. The longer you knead, the lighter the bread will be.

How to Knead Bread

1/Turn out dough on a lightly floured surface. Dough surface will be rough and sticky.

2/Knead dough, adding flour as necessary, until surface is smooth. Dough should be elastic and no longer sticky.

RISING

The kneaded dough is coated with shortening to prevent surface drying. Then it is set in a warm place to rise. The warmth encourages the yeast to grow and produce carbon dioxide. This forms bubbles in the dough, causing the dough to rise.

Yeast dough needs a room temperature of 75 to 85F (25 to 30C) for rising. In the summer, any out-of-the-way counter top will do. Dough will rise quickly. Winter provides a challenge to find a warm place. The bowl of dough may be placed in two inches of warm water, in a warm oven or near a heat source, such as a room heater or radiator. The easiest and most efficient method is to use the oven. Warm an electric oven 1 minute. Turn off oven. Place the bowl of dough in the warm oven and keep the door closed. With a gas oven, a pilot light will provide enough heat. Pre-warming a gas oven is not necessary.

Bread dough rises twice: once in the bowl and again after being shaped into a loaf. Allow dough to rise in the bowl until it doubles in size. This may take 1-1/2 to 2-1/2 hours or more, depending upon the surrounding temperature. Punch down dough by pushing your fist into the center; pull edges of dough over center. Turn out dough on a lightly floured board or work surface to knead. Punching down the dough releases some air and distributes what is left so no pockets remain to cause holes in the baked bread.

A loaf may be shaped by folding the sides under and rolling the dough between your hands into a smooth, oblong loaf. Another method is to roll out dough with a rolling pin into a rectangle the length of the bread pan and twice its width. Roll up the dough, jelly-roll fashion. Pinch seam closed and fold ends under. Place loaf in a greased bread pan. Pan should be no more than half full.

Let dough rise again in the pan until nearly doubled in size. This will take about half as much time as the first rising. Gently touch a corner of the loaf. It should feel light and an indentation will remain.

BAKING

Baking kills yeast and sets the bread structure. Breads made with milk and sugar will form a crisp, golden crust during baking. Those made with water and little or no sugar do not brown. Glazes brushed on the bread before and sometimes during baking can create the desired crust.

Egg glazes can be whole egg, egg yolk or egg white. Water or milk is usually beaten into the egg to make the glaze easy to brush. Egg glazes give bread a crisp, shiny, deeply browned crust.

Milk brushed on the loaf makes a crisp, brown crust that is dull rather than shiny. Butter or margarine is applied during the last five minutes of baking for a soft, browned crust.

A thickened cornstarch glaze is brushed on French-style breads before and during baking. The baked bread has an extra-crisp, chewy crust that is lightly browned and shiny.

Bread is done when it is browned appropriately for the type of bread and it sounds hollow when tapped with your fingers. The sound should compare to that made by tapping the inside of your wrist. Turn bread out of pan immediately after removing from the oven. Cool it completely on a wire rack. Bread left to cool in the pan will become soft and soggy on the bottom.

Fresh-baked bread makes the best sandwiches and is also good served plain with a bowl of soup. If used the same day it is baked, bread has a crisp crust and soft, moist interior. With storage, the crust will soften.

Be sure bread is completely cool before slicing. Allow the loaf to set at least two hours. Use a long serrated knife and a gentle sawing motion or an electric knife. Cut slices for making sandwiches 1/4 to 1/2 inch thick.

The breads that follow make super sandwiches, from simple peanut-butter and jelly to Turkey-Orange Open-Face. Most of the breads are similar to types you can find in bakeries or supermarkets. Substitute these commercial breads when you don't have time for bread-baking.

Home-Style White Bread

Makes a loaf for sandwiches and eight buns.

1/4 cup warm water (105F, 40C)
1 (1/4-oz.) pkg. active dry yeast
   (1 tablespoon)
3 tablespoons honey
2 cups milk

1/4 cup butter or margarine
2 teaspoons salt
4 cups all-purpose flour
2 to 2-1/2 cups bread flour or
   all-pupose flour

Pour 1/4 cup warm water into a small bowl; stir in yeast and 1 tablespoon honey until dissolved. Set aside until foamy, about 15 minutes. Heat milk and butter or margarine in a small saucepan until bubbles form around edge of pan; pour into a large bowl. Cool to 105F (40C) or until a few drops on your wrist feel warm. Add yeast mixture, remaining 2 tablespoons honey, salt and 3 cups all-purpose flour; beat until smooth. Cover with a dry cloth. Set aside 20 minutes. Add remaining 1 cup all-purpose flour and bread flour or all-purpose flour, 1/2 cup at a time, until dough pulls away from side of bowl. Turn out on a lightly floured board. Knead dough, adding flour as necessary, until smooth and elastic. Clean and grease bowl. Place dough in bowl, turning to grease all sides. Cover with a dry cloth. Let rise in a warm place until doubled in size, about 2 hours. Punch down dough by pushing your fist into center; pull edges of dough over center. Turn out dough on a lightly floured surface. Knead 5 times. Divide dough in half. Grease 2 (9" x 5") loaf pans. Shape each dough half into a loaf. Place in greased pans. Cover with a dry cloth. Let rise until light, about 45 minutes. Preheat oven to 375F (190C). Bake until golden brown and loaves sound hollow when tapped with your fingers, 30 to 35 minutes. Immediately remove from pans. Cool on a rack. Makes 2 loaves.

Variation

Hot-Dog Buns: Photo on page 45.
Prepare dough as above. After first rising, divide dough into 16 equal parts. Shape each part into a 6-inch-long bun by rolling dough between your hands. Place buns on a greased baking sheet at least 2 inches apart. Flatten buns slightly by rolling over them with a rolling pin. Cover with a dry cloth. Let rise until light, about 30 minutes. Preheat oven to 375F (190C). In a small bowl, beat 1 egg and 2 tablespoons milk. Brush buns with egg mixture. Bake until golden brown, about 20 minutes. Immediately remove from baking sheet. Cool on a rack. Makes 16 buns.
Hamburger Buns: Prepare dough as above. After first rising, divide dough into 16 equal parts. Shape each part into a smooth ball. Place balls on a greased baking sheet at least 2 inches apart. Flatten buns slightly by rolling over them with a rolling pin. Proceed as for Hot-Dog Buns, above. Makes 16 buns.

Special Hamburger Sauce

Great on sandwiches too, like Classic Reuben, page 118, or seafood sandwiches.

1 cup mayonnaise
2 tablespoons chili sauce
1 tablespoon ketchup
1 teaspoon prepared mustard

1 tablespoon finely chopped green bell pepper
1 tablespoon finely chopped dill pickle
1 teaspoon grated onion
1/2 teaspoon paprika

In a small bowl, combine all ingredients. Store in an airtight container in refrigerator up to 1 week. Makes about 1-1/2 cups.

Mango Chutney

Make in the summer when mangoes are in the supermarkets.

1/2 lemon	1/4 teaspoon hot red-pepper flakes
3/4 cup cider vinegar	3 firm, half-ripe mangoes
1 cup packed brown sugar	1/2 large ripe papaya
1 small garlic clove, minced	1/2 cup seedless raisins
1/2 teaspoon salt	1/4 cup coarsely chopped onion
1 tablespoon plus 1-1/2 teaspoons grated fresh gingerroot	

Peel lemon, removing colored peel and white pith. Slice lemon; chop coarsely. In a large saucepan, combine lemon, vinegar, brown sugar, garlic, salt and ginger. Add pepper flakes to vinegar mixture. Bring to a boil. Cover and simmer 30 minutes. Peel mangoes; slice flesh thinly. Scoop out seeds from papaya; discard. Peel papaya; cut flesh in 1/2-inch cubes. Add mango slices, papaya cubes, raisins and onion to vinegar mixture. Simmer, uncovered, stirring occasionally, until fruit is tender and mixture is thick, about 30 minutes. Ladle chutney into 2 to 3 (8- to 12-ounce) jars with tight-fitting lids. Store in refrigerator. Chutney will keep at least 6 months. Makes about 3 cups.

Caraway-Cheese Spread

Spread on rye bread to jazz up an ordinary ham sandwich, shown opposite.

1 (3-oz.) pkg. cream cheese, room temperature	2 cups shredded Monterey Jack cheese (8 oz.)
1/4 cup dry white wine	1 tablespoon caraway seeds

Combine cream cheese and wine in a medium bowl. Beat with an electric mixer until smooth. Add shredded cheese and caraway seeds to cream-cheese mixture. Stir until combined. Store in an airtight container in refrigerator up to 1 week. Allow to soften at room temperature 15 to 20 minutes before using. Makes about 1 cup.

Chili-Avocado Spread

Keep covered until ready to serve because surface will darken when exposed to air.

1 large avocado	1 tablespoon chili sauce
1 green onion, including 1 inch of green top, sliced	1/8 teaspoon salt
2 tablespoons dairy sour cream	1 tablespoon sliced green onion, if desired
2 teaspoons lime or lemon juice	

Peel avocado; cut flesh in pieces. In a blender or food processor, puree avocado pieces, 1 green onion, sour cream and lime or lemon juice. Spoon avocado mixture into a bowl. Stir in chili sauce and salt. Cover and refrigerate until ready to use. To serve, sprinkle with 1 tablespoon green onion, if desired. Serve within 2 hours. Makes about 1 cup.

Shown clockwise, starting from the top: Mango Chutney; Caraway-Cheese Spread; and Chili-Avocado Spread.

Poppy-Seed Egg Braids   *Photo on page 45.*

Watch carefully as bread bakes, because loaves brown quickly!

1/4 cup warm water (105F, 40C)	3 eggs, beaten
1 (1/4-oz.) pkg. active dry yeast	2-1/2 cups all-purpose flour
(1 tablespoon)	2-1/2 to 3 cups bread flour or
1 teaspoon sugar	all-purpose flour
1 cup milk	1 egg yolk
1/4 cup butter or margarine	2 tablespoons milk
2 tablespoons sugar	2 tablespoons poppy seeds
1 teaspoon salt	

Pour 1/4 cup warm water into a small bowl; stir in yeast and 1 teaspoon sugar until dissolved. Set aside until foamy, about 15 minutes. Heat 1 cup milk in a small saucepan until bubbles form around edge of pan. Cut butter or margarine into 4 pieces; add to milk. Stir in 2 tablespoons sugar and salt. Pour milk mixture into a large bowl. Cool to 105F (40C) or until a few drops on your wrist feel warm. Add yeast mixture, eggs and 2-1/2 cups all-purpose flour; beat until smooth. Cover with a dry cloth. Set aside 20 minutes. Add bread flour or all-purpose flour, 1/2 cup at a time, until dough pulls away from side of bowl. Turn out on a lightly floured board. Knead dough, adding flour as necessary, until smooth and elastic. Clean and grease bowl. Place dough in bowl, turning to grease all sides. Cover with a dry cloth. Let rise in a warm place until doubled in size, about 2 hours. Punch down dough by pushing your fist into center; pull edges of dough over center. Turn out dough on a lightly floured surface. Knead 5 times. Divide dough into 8 equal parts. Grease 2 baking sheets. Roll each piece of dough with your hands to form a 12-inch rope. Place 4 ropes, side-by-side lengthwise, on a greased baking sheet. At far end or top, pinch 4 rope-ends together. Braid, lifting far right rope over next rope, under third rope and over fourth rope. Repeat, starting each time with far right rope. Braid to end of ropes. Pinch ends together and fold under. Repeat braiding with remaining 4 ropes. In a small bowl, beat egg yolk with 2 tablespoons milk. Brush egg mixture over braids. Sprinkle generously with poppy seeds; press seeds into braids. Cover with a dry cloth. Let rise until light, about 45 minutes. Preheat oven to 350F (175C). Bake until golden brown and loaves sound hollow when tapped with your fingers, about 30 minutes. Immediately remove from baking sheets. Cool on a rack. Makes 2 loaves.

Savory Butter

Adds a classic taste to Reuben sandwiches. Also good on roast-beef sandwiches.

1/2 cup butter or margarine,	1/2 teaspoon Worcestershire sauce
room temperature	1/4 teaspoon paprika
1/8 teaspoon garlic powder	Salt to taste
1/2 teaspoon dry mustard	

In a small bowl, beat butter or margarine with an electric mixer until softened. Add garlic powder, mustard, Worcestershire sauce and paprika. Beat until light and fluffy. Season to taste with salt. Store in an airtight container in refrigerator up to 6 weeks. Allow to soften at room temperature 15 to 20 minutes before using. Makes about 1/2 cup.

Fruit-Nut Bread   Photo on page 45.

Use different dried fruits to make a variety of breads.

2/3 cup raisins or cut-up dried fruit,
   such as dates, dried apricots,
   prunes or dried apples
1/2 medium orange, sliced
3/4 cup water
1/4 cup shortening
2/3 cup sugar
1 egg

1 teaspoon vanilla extract
2 cups sifted all-purpose flour
2 teaspoons baking powder
1/4 teaspoon baking soda
1/2 teaspoon salt
1/2 cup chopped nuts such as walnuts,
   almonds, pistachios or pecans

Combine dried fruit, orange slices and water in a saucepan; bring to a boil. Cover pan and set aside 15 minutes. Grease a 9'' x 5'' loaf pan or thoroughly wash, dry and grease a 1-pound coffee can. Preheat oven to 350F (175C). In a mixing bowl, beat shortening, sugar, egg and vanilla with electric mixer until fluffy. Sift together flour, baking powder, baking soda and salt. Remove orange slices from fruit mixture; squeeze slices over saucepan to remove juice. Stir fruit mixture and nuts into sugar mixture. Add flour mixture all at once. Stir gently until flour is moistened. Turn batter into greased pan or can. Bake until a wooden pick inserted in center of loaf comes out clean, about 50 minutes. Cool in pan 10 minutes. Remove from pan; cool on a rack. For easier slicing, store loaf overnight before slicing. Makes 1 loaf.

Cinnamon Butter

Try on warm slices of Fruit-Nut Bread, above.

1/2 cup butter or margarine,
   room temperature
1/4 cup packed brown sugar

1 teaspoon ground cinnamon
1/8 teaspoon ground nutmeg
1/2 cup finely chopped walnuts

In a small bowl, beat butter or margarine with an electric mixer until softened. Beat in brown sugar, cinnamon and nutmeg until light and fluffy. Stir in walnuts. Store in an airtight container in refrigerator up to 6 weeks. Allow to soften at room temperature 15 to 20 minutes before using. Makes about 3/4 cup.

Sesame-Nut Butter

No additional oil is necessary when using roasted nuts.

1/2 cup sesame seeds
2 cups roasted cashews

1 cup roasted hulled sunflower seeds
1 teaspoon honey

Toast sesame seeds in a heavy skillet over medium heat, stirring constantly, until golden brown. Quickly remove seeds from skillet to prevent burning. Combine cashews and sunflower seeds in a blender or food processor. Process on high speed until smooth. Scrape down sides often. Add honey; blend in. Place mixture in a small bowl. Stir in toasted sesame seeds. Store in a jar or air-tight container in refrigerator or at room temperature up to 2 months. Makes about 2 cups.

Cheddar-Cheese Bread   *Photo on page 45.*

A very flavorful bread for meat and salad sandwiches.

1/4 cup warm water (105F, 40C)
1 (1/4-oz.) pkg. active dry yeast
  (1 tablespoon)
1 teaspoon sugar
2 cups warm water (105F, 40C)
2/3 cup non-fat dry milk powder

2 tablespoons vegetable oil
1 teaspoon salt
3 cups all-purpose flour
3 to 3-1/2 cups bread flour or
  all-purpose flour
3 cups shredded Cheddar cheese (12 oz.)

Pour 1/4 cup warm water into a small bowl; stir in yeast and sugar until dissolved. Set aside until foamy, about 15 minutes. Pour 2 cups warm water into a large bowl. Stir in milk powder, oil and salt until milk powder dissolves. Add yeast mixture and 3 cups all-purpose flour; beat until smooth. Cover with a dry cloth. Set aside 20 minutes. Add bread flour or all-purpose flour, 1/2 cup at a time, until dough pulls away from side of bowl. Turn out on a lightly floured board. Knead dough, adding flour as necessary, until smooth and elastic. Clean and grease bowl. Place dough in bowl, turning to grease all sides. Cover with a dry cloth. Let rise in a warm place until doubled in size, about 2 hours. Punch down dough by pushing your fist into center; pull edges of dough over center. Turn out dough on a lightly floured surface. Knead 5 times. Divide dough in half. Grease 2 (9" x 5") loaf pans. Roll out each half of dough to a 15" x 12" rectangle. Sprinkle 1-1/2 cups cheese over each rectangle. Beginning at 12-inch side, roll up jelly-roll fashion. With seam-side down, roll out to an 18" x 6" rectangle. Cut dough lengthwise in 3 (2-inch-wide) strips. Turn each strip, cut-side up. Braid strips, keeping cut-sides up. Place braid in greased pan, folding ends under. Repeat with other rectangle. Cover with a dry cloth. Let rise until light, about 45 minutes. Preheat oven to 350F (175C). Bake until browned and loaves sound hollow when tapped with your fingers, 30 to 35 minutes. Immediately remove from pans. Cool on a rack. Makes 2 loaves.

Garden-Vegetable Spread

Beau Monde and Bon Appétit are similar seasoning salts. Use either one.

1 (3-oz.) pkg. cream cheese,
  room temperature
1/4 cup dairy sour cream
1 teaspoon Beau Monde or
  Bon Appétit seasoning

1/4 teaspoon curry powder
1 green onion, chopped
1 tablespoon shredded carrot
1 tablespoon minced celery
1 tablespoon minced green bell pepper

Beat cream cheese in a small bowl with an electric mixer until smooth. Beat in sour cream, Beau Monde or Bon Appétit seasoning and curry powder until fluffy. Stir in green onion, carrot, celery and green pepper. Store in an airtight container in refrigerator up to 2 days. Allow to soften at room temperature 15 to 20 minutes before using. Makes about 1/2 cup.

How to Make Cheddar-Cheese Bread

1/Roll out each half of dough to a 15" x 12" rectangle. Sprinkle 1-1/2 cups cheese over each rectangle. Beginning at 12-inch side, roll up dough, jelly-roll fashion.

2/With seam-side down, roll out each cheese-filled roll to an 18" x 6" rectangle. Cut lengthwise in 3 strips. Turn each strip cut-side up and braid strips.

Festive Chili Butter

When using fresh garlic, the flavor intensifies the longer the butter is stored.

1/2 cup butter or margarine,
   room temperature
1 garlic clove, minced, or
   1/8 teaspoon garlic powder

1 teaspoon chili powder
1/8 teaspoon ground cumin
1 tablespoon finely chopped green onion
Salt to taste

In a small bowl, beat butter or margarine with an electric mixer until softened. Beat in garlic or garlic powder, chili powder, cumin and green onion. Season to taste with salt. Store in an airtight container in refrigerator up to 3 days. Allow to soften at room temperature 15 to 20 minutes before using. Makes about 1/2 cup.

Champagne Mustard

Specialty food stores and some supermarkets sell champagne vinegar.

1 cup dry white champagne
2 cups champagne vinegar or
   white-wine vinegar
1 cup chopped onion
2 garlic cloves, minced

1 (4-oz.) can dry mustard
1/4 cup sugar
2 teaspoons cornstarch
2 teaspoons salt
2 eggs, well beaten

In a medium saucepan, combine champagne, vinegar, onion and garlic. Bring to a boil; reduce heat. Cover and simmer 5 minutes. Remove from heat. Cool 2 hours. Strain champagne mixture into a 1-quart measuring cup or bowl. Discard onion and garlic. Combine mustard, sugar, cornstarch and salt in top of a double boiler. Using a whisk, gradually blend in champagne mixture. Beat eggs into mixture. Cook over hot but not boiling water, beating constantly, until thickened, about 15 minutes. Ladle mustard into 3 (8- to 12-ounce) jars with tight-fitting lids. Store in refrigerator. Mustard will keep at least 9 months. Makes about 3 cups.

How to Make Champagne Mustard

1/Strain champagne mixture into a 1-quart measuring cup or bowl. Discard onion and garlic.

2/Cook mixture over hot water, beating constantly, until thickened. Ladle mustard into storage jars.

Bagels

Boiling in sugar water before baking gives bagels a crisp, brown, chewy crust.

1-1/2 cups warm water (105F, 40C)	**1 tablespoon butter or margarine, melted**
1 (1/4-oz.) pkg. active dry yeast	**4-1/2 to 5 cups all-purpose flour**
(1 tablespoon)	**2 qts. water**
2 tablespoons sugar	**2 tablespoons sugar**
1 teaspoon salt	

Pour 1-1/2 cups warm water into a large bowl; stir in yeast and 2 tablespoons sugar until dissolved. Set aside until foamy, about 15 minutes. Add salt, butter or margarine and 2 cups flour; beat until smooth. Cover with a dry cloth; set aside 20 minutes. Add remaining flour, 1 cup at a time, until dough pulls away from side of bowl. Turn out on a lightly floured board. Knead dough, adding flour as necessary, until smooth and elastic. Dough should be firmer than most bread dough, but not stiff or dry. Clean and grease bowl. Place dough in bowl, turning to grease all sides. Cover with a dry cloth. Let rise in a warm place until doubled in size, about 2 hours. Punch down dough by pushing your fist into center; pull edges of dough over center. Turn out dough on a lightly floured surface. Knead 5 times. Divide dough into 18 equal parts. Roll each part into an 8-inch rope. Form rope into a circle, crossing rope about 1/2 inch from ends. Pinch together; fold ends under. Pinch again. Place bagels on lightly floured baking sheets. Cover with a dry cloth. Let rise 20 minutes. Preheat oven to 400F (205C). Grease 3 baking sheets. In a 4- or 6-quart pot, boil 2 quarts water and 2 tablespoons sugar. Carefully slip 4 or 5 bagels at a time into boiling water. Boil about 1 minute, turning frequently. If bagels boil too long, they will become soggy. Remove with slotted spoon. Place on greased baking sheets. Bake boiled bagels until lightly browned, 15 to 20 minutes. Immediately remove from baking sheets. Cool on a rack. Makes 18 bagels.

Variations

Whole-Wheat Bagels: Substitute 2 tablespoons honey for 2 tablespoons sugar combined with yeast. Substitute 2 cups whole-wheat flour for 2 cups of all-purpose flour.
Corn-Rye Bagels: Photo on page 45.
Substitute 2 tablespoons molasses for 2 tablespoons sugar combined with yeast. Substitute 1 cup rye flour, 1 cup whole-wheat flour, 1/2 cup cornmeal and 1-1/2 to 2 cups all-purpose flour for 4-1/2 to 5 cups all-purpose flour. Stir 1 tablespoon caraway seeds into dough when adding flour.

Lemon-Pepper Butter

Adds a flavor bonus to cold-cut sandwiches.

1/2 cup butter or margarine,	**2 tablespoons finely chopped fresh parsley**
room temperature	**1 teaspoon finely chopped chives or**
1 teaspoon lemon juice	**green onion**
1/2 teaspoon grated lemon peel	**1/4 teaspoon coarsely ground black pepper**

In a small bowl, beat butter or margarine with an electric mixer until softened. Add remaining ingredients. Beat until light and fluffy. Store in an airtight container in refrigerator up to 3 days. Allow to soften at room temperature 15 to 20 minutes before using. Makes about 1/2 cup.

Squaw Bread   *Photo on pages 45 and 117.*

An American-Indian bread that is dark and slightly sweet with a glossy crust.

1/4 cup warm water (105F, 40C)	2 teaspoons salt
1 (1/4-oz.) pkg. active dry yeast	1 cup whole-wheat flour
(1 tablespoon)	1 cup rye flour
1 teaspoon sugar	3 to 3-1/2 cups bread flour or
1 cup buttermilk	all-purpose flour
1/4 cup butter or margarine, melted	Cornmeal
3/4 cup warm water (105F, 40C)	1 egg
1/2 cup molasses	2 tablespoons milk

Pour 1/4 cup warm water into a small bowl; stir in yeast and sugar until dissolved. Set aside until foamy, about 15 minutes. Heat buttermilk in a small saucepan until warm. Stir in butter or margarine, 3/4 cup warm water, molasses and salt. Pour buttermilk mixture into a large bowl. Add yeast mixture, whole-wheat flour, rye flour and 1 cup bread flour or all-purpose flour; beat until smooth. Cover with a dry cloth. Set aside 20 minutes. Add remaining bread flour or all-purpose flour, 1/2 cup at a time, until dough pulls away from side of bowl. Turn out on a lightly floured board. Knead dough, adding flour as necessary, until smooth and elastic. Clean and grease bowl. Place dough in bowl, turning to grease all sides. Cover with a dry cloth. Let rise in a warm place until doubled in size, about 2 hours. Punch down dough by pushing your fist into center; pull edges of dough over center. Turn out dough on a lightly floured surface. Knead 5 times. Divide dough in half. Grease 2 round 8-inch baking pans. Sprinkle generously with cornmeal. Shape each half of dough into a smooth ball. Place a ball of dough in each greased pan. Cover with a dry cloth. Let rise until light, about 45 minutes. Preheat oven to 375F (190C). In a small bowl, beat egg and milk. Brush egg mixture on loaves. With a razor blade or sharp knife, cut an "X" in top of each loaf. Bake until browned and loaves sound hollow when tapped with your fingers, about 40 minutes. Immediately remove from pans. Cool on a rack. Makes 2 loaves.

Fruit & Nut Butter

Hulled sunflower seeds, peanuts and dried fruit make a different nut spread.

4 cups dry-roasted unsalted peanuts	1/2 cup chopped raisins, dates or
1/2 cup roasted hulled sunflower seeds	dried apricots
2 to 3 tablespoons peanut oil or	Salt, if desired
other light-flavored vegetable oil	
1 tablespoon honey	

Combine peanuts and sunflower seeds in a blender or food processor. Process on high speed until coarsely chopped. Scrape down sides often. Continue processing, adding oil in a thin stream, until smooth. Add honey; blend in. Place mixture in a small bowl. Stir in chopped raisins or other dried fruit. Season with salt, if desired. Store in a jar or airtight container in refrigerator or at room temperature up to 2 months. Makes about 2 cups.

Russian Black Bread

Chocolate and coffee give a rich, dark color and add a subtle flavor.

1/4 cup warm water (105F, 40C)
1 (1/4-oz.) pkg. active dry yeast
  (1 tablespoon)
1 teaspoon sugar
1 cup boiling water
1 cup raisins
2 tablespoons vegetable oil
1 teaspoon salt

2 tablespoons dark molasses
1 oz. unsweetened chocolate, melted
1 teaspoon instant-coffee powder
1-1/2 cups rye flour
2 to 2-1/2 cups bread flour or
  all-purpose flour
1 teaspoon cornstarch
1/2 cup cold water

Pour 1/4 cup warm water into a small bowl; stir in yeast and sugar until dissolved. Set aside until foamy, about 15 minutes. In a large bowl, pour boiling water over raisins. Cool to 105F (40C) or until a few drops on your wrist feel warm. Stir in oil, salt, molasses, chocolate, coffee and yeast mixture. Add rye flour; beat until smooth. Cover with a dry cloth. Set aside 20 minutes. Add bread flour or all-purpose flour, 1/2 cup at a time, until dough pulls away from side of bowl. Turn out on a lightly floured board. Knead dough, adding flour as needed, until smooth and elastic. Clean and grease bowl. Place dough in bowl, turning to grease all sides. Cover with a dry cloth. Let rise in a warm place until doubled in size, about 2 hours. Punch down dough by pushing your fist into center; pull edges of dough over center. Turn out dough on a lightly floured surface. Knead 5 times. Grease a baking sheet. Roll out dough to a 16" x 10" rectangle. Tightly roll up rectangle, starting at the shorter side. Use your finger tips to pinch roll tight. Pinch seams together. Using the palms of your hands, press on the ends of loaf, rolling back and forth on work surface to taper ends. Place loaf, seam-side down, on greased baking sheet. Cover with a dry cloth. Let rise until light, about 45 minutes. In a small saucepan, combine cornstarch and cold water. Bring to a boil, stirring constantly. Cool mixture until slightly warm. Preheat oven to 375F (190C). Brush cornstarch mixture on loaf. Bake 20 minutes. Stir cornstarch mixture; brush on loaf again. Bake until dark brown and loaf sounds hollow when tapped with your fingers, 15 to 20 minutes longer. Immediately remove from baking sheet. Cool on a rack. Makes 1 loaf.

Devilish Butter

Great for grilled cheese sandwiches.

1/2 cup butter or margarine,
  room temperature
1 teaspoon lemon juice
1 teaspoon dry mustard

1/4 teaspoon paprika
1 to 2 drops hot-pepper sauce
Salt to taste

Place butter or margarine in a small bowl. Beat with an electric mixer until softened. Add lemon juice, mustard and paprika. Beat until light and fluffy. Season to taste with hot-pepper sauce and salt. Store in an airtight container in refrigerator up to 6 weeks. Allow to soften at room temperature 15 to 20 minutes before using. Makes about 1/2 cup.

Croissants

Light and flaky crescent-shape rolls that take time but no special skill to make.

1/2 cup warm water (105F, 40C)
1 (1/4-oz.) pkg. active dry yeast
   (1 tablespoon)
2 tablespoons sugar
1/2 cup milk
2 tablespoons butter or margarine

3/4 cup cake flour
2-1/4 cups sifted all-purpose flour
1/2 teaspoon salt
2 sticks butter or margarine (1 cup)
1 egg yolk
2 tablespoons water

Pour 1/2 cup warm water into a small bowl; stir in yeast and sugar until dissolved. Set aside until foamy, about 15 minutes. Heat milk and 2 tablespoons butter or margarine in small saucepan until butter or margarine melts. Cool to 105F (40C) or until a few drops on your wrist feel warm. In a large bowl, combine yeast mixture, milk mixture, cake flour, all-purpose flour and salt. Stir until flour is moistened. Turn out on a lightly floured surface. Knead until dough holds together and is smooth, about 30 times. Dough should be soft. Cover with a dry cloth. Let dough rest 10 minutes. Cut each stick of butter or margarine in 10 pats. Roll out dough to a 12" x 8" rectangle. Place 10 pats side by side in the center 1/3 of dough. Fold 1 side over pats; pinch edges to seal. Place remaining butter or margarine over folded 1/3. Fold remaining 1/3 of dough over top; pinch again to seal. Give dough a quarter turn. Roll dough from center away from you and from center toward you. Do not roll side to side. Roll out to a 15" x 8" rectangle. Fold in thirds again. Give dough a quarter turn; roll and fold again. Wrap in waxed paper or clean cloth. Refrigerate 15 minutes. Roll, fold and turn dough 2 more times. Cut dough in half. Refrigerate 1 hour. Turn out half of dough onto a lightly floured surface. Roll into a 14" x 8" rectangle. With a pastry cutter or long knife, cut in half crosswise and lengthwise forming 4 (7" x 4") rectangles. Cut each rectangle diagonally to form 8 triangles. Remove 1 triangle. Roll 4-inch edge until it measures 5 to 6 inches. Roll up from this edge to point of triangle. Place, point-side down, on an ungreased baking sheet. Slightly curve both ends toward center, forming a crescent. Repeat with remaining triangles. In a small bowl, beat egg yolk with water. Brush rolls with egg-yolk mixture. Do not brush cut surfaces. Let rolls rise at room temperature 45 minutes. Rolls should *not* double in size. Preheat oven to 400F (205C). Brush rolls again with egg mixture. Bake 12 to 15 minutes or until golden brown. Cool on a rack. To freeze, wrap cooled croissants in foil or freezer wrap. Freeze up to 6 weeks. To thaw, warm croissants in a 350F (175C) oven 10 minutes. Makes 16 croissants.

Maple-Honey Butter

A great midnight snack when spread on toasted Crumpets, page 51.

1/2 cup butter or margarine,
   room temperature
1 tablespoon maple syrup

1 tablespoon honey
1/2 cup finely chopped pecans

In a small bowl, beat butter or margarine with an electric mixer until softened. Beat in maple syrup and honey until fluffy. Stir in pecans. Store in an airtight container in refrigerator up to 6 weeks. Allow to soften at room temperature 15 to 20 minutes before using. Makes 3/4 cup.

Shown clockwise, starting from the top: Scots Oat Bread, page 46; Seeded Kaiser Rolls, page 48; Onion Rolls, page 50; Corn-Rye Bagels, page 41; Hot-Dog Buns, page 33; Squaw Bread, page 42; Fruit-Nut Bread, page 37; Maple-Honey Butter; Croissants; Cheddar-Pepper-Cheese Spread, page 47; Cheddar-Cheese Bread, page 38; and Poppy-Seed Egg Braid, page 36.

Scots Oat Bread   *Photo on page 45.*

Moist and tender, a perfect bread with cheese spreads.

1/4 cup warm water (105F, 40C)	2 tablespoons honey
1 (1/4-oz.) pkg. active dry yeast	2 tablespoons vegetable oil
(1 tablespoon)	1 cup quick-cooking rolled oats
1 teaspoon sugar	3 to 3-1/2 cups all-purpose flour
1/2 cup milk	2 tablespoons milk
1 cup creamed cottage cheese (8 oz.)	1 tablespoon quick-cooking rolled oats
1 teaspoon salt	

Pour 1/4 cup warm water into a small bowl; stir in yeast and sugar until dissolved. Set aside until foamy, about 15 minutes. Heat milk and cottage cheese in a small saucepan until warm. Pour milk mixture into a large bowl. Add salt, honey and vegetable oil. Cool, if necessary, to warm. Add yeast mixture, 1 cup oats and 1 cup all-purpose flour; beat until smooth. Cover with a dry cloth. Set aside 20 minutes. Add remaining all-purpose flour, 1/2 cup at a time, until dough pulls away from side of bowl. Turn out on a lightly floured board. Knead dough, adding flour as necessary, until smooth and elastic. Clean and grease bowl. Place dough in bowl, turning to grease all sides. Cover with a dry cloth. Let rise in a warm place until doubled in size, about 2 hours. Punch down dough by pushing your fist into center; pull edges of dough over center. Turn out dough on a lightly floured surface. Knead 5 times. Grease a 9" x 5" loaf pan. Shape dough into a loaf. Place in greased pan. Brush loaf with milk. Sprinkle 1 tablespoon rolled oats over top of loaf. Cover with a dry cloth. Let rise until light, about 45 minutes. Preheat oven to 375F (190C). Bake until browned and loaf sounds hollow when tapped with your fingers, 30 to 35 minutes. Immediately remove from pan. Cool on a rack. Makes 1 loaf.

Tangy-Sweet Spread

Great as a hot-dog spread!

1 (3-oz.) pkg. cream cheese,	1 tablespoon prepared mustard
room temperature	1/8 teaspoon ground ginger
1/2 cup mayonnaise	Red (cayenne) pepper to taste
1 tablespoon honey	

Beat cream cheese in a medium bowl with an electric mixer until smooth. Add mayonnaise; continue beating until light and fluffy. Beat in honey, mustard and ginger. Season to taste with red pepper. Store in an airtight container in refrigerator up to 1 week. Allow to soften at room temperature 15 to 20 minutes before using. Makes about 1 cup.

Broil sandwiches with cheese only until cheese melts. Overcooked cheese becomes tough and rubbery.

Pepper-Cheese Spread

For a milder taste, use green chilies instead of jalapeño peppers.

2 (3-oz.) pkgs. cream cheese,
  room temperature
2/3 cup milk
2 cups finely shredded Cheddar cheese
  (8 oz.)

1/4 cup finely chopped jalapeño peppers
2 tablespoons finely chopped pimiento
2 cups finely shredded Monterey Jack cheese
  (8 oz.)

Combine 1 package cream cheese and 1/3 cup milk in a medium bowl. Beat with an electric mixer until smooth. Add Cheddar cheese, 2 tablespoons jalapeño peppers and 1 tablespoon pimiento. Stir until well blended. In another bowl, combine remaining package cream cheese and 1/3 cup milk. Beat with electric mixer until smooth. Add Monterey Jack cheese, 2 tablespoons jalapeño peppers and 1 tablespoon pimiento. Stir until well blended. Spoon both cheese mixtures into 1 bowl. Stir slightly to give a swirled effect. Store in an airtight container in refrigerator up to 1 week. Allow to soften at room temperature 15 to 20 minutes before serving. Makes about 3 cups.

Variations

Monterey Jack-Pepper-Cheese Spread: Use 1 pound Monterey Jack cheese instead of combination of cheeses. Beat together both packages cream cheese and all the milk until smooth. Stir in Monterey Jack cheese, jalapeño peppers and pimiento as above.
Cheddar-Pepper-Cheese Spread: Photo on page 45.
Use 1 pound Cheddar cheese instead of combination of cheeses. Proceed as for Monterey Jack-Pepper-Cheese Spread, above.

Simple Homemade Mayonnaise

Add seasonings to basic mayonnaise for a variety of spreads.

2 egg yolks
1/4 teaspoon dry mustard
1/2 teaspoon sugar
1/2 teaspoon salt

1 tablespoon white-wine vinegar
1-1/2 to 2 cups vegetable oil
1 tablespoon lemon juice

In a deep bowl, beat together egg yolks, mustard, sugar and salt. Slowly add vinegar, beating constantly. Continue to beat while adding oil, 1 teaspoon at a time, until about 1/4 cup has been added. Add 1 tablespoon oil at a time while beating, until 1 cup oil has been added. Beat in lemon juice. Continue adding oil in a thin stream until mayonnaise reaches desired consistency. Store in a jar or airtight container in refrigerator up to 6 weeks. Makes about 2 cups.

Variation

Blender Mayonnaise: Substitute 1 whole egg for 2 egg yolks. Combine egg, mustard, sugar and salt in blender or food processor. Process until well blended. With motor running, slowly add vinegar. Process on medium speed while adding oil in a thin stream until about 1 cup oil has been added. Mayonnaise should be thick. Add lemon juice. Continue adding oil with motor running until mayonnaise reaches desired consistency. Makes about 2 cups.

Seeded Kaiser Rolls   *Photo on page 45.*

Great to use for hot or cold sandwiches.

1-1/2 cups warm water (105F, 40C)	**1 teaspoon salt**
1 (1/4-oz.) pkg. active dry yeast	**2 cups all-purpose flour**
(1 tablespoon)	**1-1/2 to 2 cups bread flour or**
1 tablespoon sugar	**all-purpose flour**
1 tablespoon butter or margarine, melted	**2 tablespoons milk**
1 egg, beaten	**1/4 cup poppy seeds or sesame seeds**

Pour 1-1/2 cups water into a large bowl; stir in yeast and sugar until dissolved. Set aside until foamy, about 15 minutes. Add 1 tablespoon butter or margarine, egg, salt and 2 cups all-purpose flour; beat until smooth. Cover with a dry cloth. Set aside 20 minutes. Add bread flour or all-purpose flour, 1/2 cup at a time, until dough pulls away from side of bowl. Turn out on a lightly floured board. Knead dough, adding flour as necessary, until smooth and elastic. Clean and grease bowl. Place dough in bowl, turning to grease all sides. Cover with a dry cloth. Let rise in a warm place until doubled in size, about 2 hours. Punch down dough by pushing your fist into center; pull edges of dough over center. Turn out dough on a lightly floured surface. Knead 5 times. Divide dough into 8 equal pieces. Grease 2 baking sheets. Roll each piece of dough into a 10-inch rope. Tie each rope in a knot. Tuck 1 end of rope into center of knot. Turn other end under knot. Place rolls on greased baking sheet. Brush rolls with milk. Sprinkle generously with poppy seeds or sesame seeds; press seeds into rolls. Cover with a dry cloth. Let rise until light, about 45 minutes. Preheat oven to 375F (190C). Bake until golden brown and rolls sound hollow when tapped with your fingers, about 20 minutes. Immediately remove from baking sheets. Cool on a rack. Makes 8 rolls.

Spicy Tomato Mustard

Perks up a bologna or salami sandwich.

1 cup distilled white vinegar	**2 tablespoons honey**
1 (8-oz.) can tomato sauce	**2 teaspoons salt**
1 (4-oz.) can dry mustard	**1/4 teaspoon ground turmeric**
1 tablespoon vegetable oil	**1/4 teaspoon ground allspice**
1 cup chopped onion	**1/4 teaspoon ground cloves**

Stir together vinegar and tomato sauce in a bowl. Place mustard in a medium saucepan. Gradually add vinegar mixture to mustard, beating constantly with a whisk; set aside. Heat oil in a small skillet. Add onion; sauté until tender. Add sautéed onion, honey, salt, turmeric, allspice and cloves to mustard mixture; stir well. Cook mixture over medium-low heat, stirring constantly, until thickened, about 20 minutes. Ladle mustard into 2 or 3 (8- to 12-ounce) jars with tight-fitting lids. Store in refrigerator. Mustard will keep at least 9 months. Makes about 2 cups.

*For information on processing mustards and chutneys for longer storage, see **Canning** by Sue & Bill Deeming, published by HPBooks.*

How to Make Seeded Kaiser Rolls

1/Tie each dough rope in a knot. Tuck 1 end of rope into center of knot. Turn other end under knot. Place rolls on greased baking sheet.

2/Brush shaped rolls with milk. Sprinkle generously with poppy seeds or sesame seeds. Press seeds into rolls. Cover and let rise.

Horseradish-Cream Sauce

A mild tasting horseradish sauce that's great with roast-beef sandwiches.

1/2 cup mayonnaise	1/4 teaspoon salt
1/4 cup dairy sour cream	1/8 teaspoon paprika
1 tablespoon prepared horseradish	

Combine mayonnaise and sour cream in a small bowl. Stir in horseradish. Season with salt and paprika. Store in an airtight container in refrigerator up to 1 week. Makes about 3/4 cup.

Onion Rolls   *Photo on page 45.*

Pureed onion in the dough carries the flavor throughout the rolls.

1/4 cup warm water (105F, 40C)
1 (1/4-oz.) pkg. active dry yeast
  (1 tablespoon)
1 teaspoon sugar
1 cup hot water
1/3 cup non-fat dry milk powder
1 tablespoon sugar
1 teaspoon salt

1 small onion, chopped
2 tablespoons water
1 tablespoon vegetable oil
1 egg, beaten
2 cups all-purpose flour
1-1/2 to 2 cups bread flour or
  all-purpose flour
1/2 tablespoon butter or margarine

Pour 1/4 cup warm water into a small bowl; stir in yeast and 1 teaspoon sugar until dissolved. Set aside until foamy, about 15 minutes. In a large bowl, combine 1 cup hot water, milk powder, 1 tablespoon sugar and salt. Puree 1/4 cup chopped onion and 2 tablespoons water in a blender. Reserve remaining onion. Strain pureed onion through a fine sieve, discarding liquid. Heat oil in a small skillet. Add pureed onion; sauté 1 minute. Add sautéed onion to milk mixture. Add beaten egg, yeast mixture and 2 cups all-purpose flour; beat until smooth. Cover with a dry cloth. Set aside 20 minutes. Add bread flour or all-purpose flour, 1/2 cup at a time, until dough pulls away from side of bowl. Turn out on a lightly floured board. Knead dough, adding flour as necessary, until smooth and elastic. Clean and grease bowl. Place dough in bowl, turning to grease all sides. Cover with a dry cloth. Let rise in a warm place until doubled in size, about 2 hours. Punch down dough by pushing your fist into center; pull edges of dough over center. Turn out dough on a lightly floured surface. Knead 5 times. Divide dough into 8 equal parts. Grease 2 baking sheets. Shape each part of dough into a smooth ball. Place on baking sheet. Flatten rolls by rolling over each with a rolling pin. Heat butter or margarine in small skillet. Add reserved chopped onion; sauté until tender. Spread sautéed onion over top of rolls. Cover with a dry cloth. Let rise until light, about 30 minutes. Preheat oven to 375F (190C). Bake until lightly browned, about 20 minutes. Immediately remove from baking sheet. Cool on a rack. Makes 8 rolls.

Variation

Onion-Bacon Rolls: Prepare dough as directed. Shape into rolls. Fry 3 bacon slices in a small skillet until crisp. Drain on paper towels. Crumble bacon. Remove all but 1/2 tablespoon bacon drippings from skillet. Add onion; sauté until tender. Spread onion on top of rolls. Sprinkle crumbled bacon over rolls. Press onion and bacon into rolls. Let rolls rise. Bake as directed above.

Storing Bread

Bread keeps longer if stored unsliced. Place cooled loaf in a plastic bag and store at room temperature. Homemade bread will stay fresh two to three days, if not eaten before then! When baking several loaves at a time, freeze bread that won't be eaten right away. Wrap cooled loaves in foil, freezer paper or freezer bags. Do not use ordinary bread bags or plastic bags. They do not prevent moisture loss. Frozen bread can be stored in the freezer up to three months at 0F (−20C). If stored in the freezer compartment of a refrigerator, plan to store bread only two to three weeks. Constant opening and closing causes the temperature to vary, thus shortening storage time.

English-Muffin Bread

Bake in a can, slice thick and use like English muffins.

1/4 cup warm water (105F, 40C)
1 (1/4-oz.) pkg. active dry yeast
   (1 tablespoon)
1 teaspoon sugar
1 cup milk

1 egg, beaten
1 teaspoon salt
3 to 3-1/2 cups all-purpose flour
1 cup raisins, if desired
Cornmeal

Pour 1/4 cup warm water into a small bowl; stir in yeast and sugar until dissolved. Set aside until foamy, about 15 minutes. Heat milk in a small saucepan until small bubbles form around edge of pan. Pour milk into a large bowl. Cool to 105F (40C) or until a few drops on your wrist feel warm. Add beaten egg, salt, yeast mixture and 1-1/2 cups all-purpose flour; beat until smooth. Cover with a dry cloth. Set aside 20 minutes. Add remaining all-purpose flour, 1/2 cup at a time, until dough pulls away from side of bowl. Stir in raisins, if desired. Dough should be hard to beat with a wooden spoon but too sticky to handle. Beat vigorously with spoon until smooth, about 5 minutes. Thoroughly wash, dry and grease 2 (1-pound) coffee cans. Sprinkle insides of cans with cornmeal. Spoon half the dough into each can. Sprinkle top with cornmeal. Cover with a dry cloth. Let rise in a warm place until doubled in size, about 1 hour. Preheat oven to 375F (190C). Bake 30 minutes or until lightly browned. Immediately remove from cans. Cool on a rack. Makes 2 loaves.

Variation

Cornmeal-English-Muffin Bread: Substitute 3/4 cup cornmeal and 1-3/4 to 2-1/4 cups all-purpose flour for 3 to 3-1/2 cups all-purpose flour.

Crumpets

The English serve these toasted with butter and jam. They are also good in a variety of sandwiches.

1/4 cup warm water (105F, 40C)
1 teaspoon active dry yeast
1 tablespoon sugar
2/3 cup milk
1 egg, beaten

2 cups all-purpose flour
1 teaspoon salt
1/2 teaspoon baking soda
1/4 cup warm water (105F, 40C)

Pour 1/4 cup warm water into a small bowl; stir in yeast and sugar until dissolved. Set aside until foamy, about 15 minutes. Heat milk in a small saucepan until bubbles form around edge of pan; pour milk into a large bowl. Cool to 105F (40C) or until a few drops on your wrist feel warm. Add egg and yeast mixture to milk; stir until combined. Add flour and salt; beat until smooth and elastic, about 3 minutes. Cover with a dry cloth. Let rise in a warm place until batter has doubled in size and surface is a mass of bubbles, about 1-1/2 hours. In a small bowl, stir baking soda into 1/4 cup warm water until dissolved. Stir soda mixture into batter. Cover bowl with a cloth. Set aside 30 minutes. Lightly grease a griddle and 3 or 4 crumpet rings. Tuna cans with top and bottom removed may be used for crumpet rings. If using tuna cans, bake in a 350F (175C) oven 20 minutes to sterilize; remove and cool completely. Place rings on griddle. Heat over medium-low heat until quite warm. Pour batter into rings no more than 1/2 inch deep. Cook until surface forms a dull skin and tiny holes cover the surface, 8 to 10 minutes. Slip off rings; turn crumpets. Cook 1 minute longer. Cool on a rack. Makes 8 to 10.

Cucumber-Yogurt Sauce

Refreshing sauce to spoon over sandwiches such as Felafel, page 128.

1 large cucumber, peeled, shredded	**1 teaspoon lemon juice**
1/2 teaspoon salt	**1/8 teaspoon garlic salt**
1 (8-oz.) carton plain yogurt (1 cup)	**1 tablespoon minced fresh parsley or**
1/2 cup mayonnaise	**1 teaspoon dried leaf parsley**

Spread shredded cucumber on a cloth towel. Sprinkle with salt. Let stand 30 minutes. Bring the ends of towel together. Squeeze moisture out of cucumber. In a small bowl, combine yogurt and mayonnaise. Stir in cucumber, lemon juice, garlic salt and parsley. Store in an airtight container in refrigerator up to 2 days. Makes about 1-1/2 cups.

How to Make Cucumber-Yogurt Sauce

1/Spread cucumber on towel. Sprinkle with salt. Let stand 30 minutes.

2/Bring ends of towel together. Squeeze moisture out of cucumber.

Crusty French Bread

Gluten flour can be purchased in health-food stores. A substitute is all-purpose flour.

1-1/2 cups warm water (105F, 40C)
1 (1/4-oz.) pkg. active dry yeast
  (1 tablespoon)
1 tablespoon sugar
1 teaspoon salt
1 tablespoon butter or margarine, melted

1 cup gluten flour
2-1/2 to 3 cups all-purpose flour
2 tablespoons cornmeal
1 teaspoon cornstarch
1/2 cup cold water

Pour 1-1/2 cups warm water into a large bowl; stir in yeast and sugar until dissolved. Set aside until foamy, about 15 minutes. Add salt, butter or margarine, gluten flour and 1 cup all-purpose flour; beat until smooth. Cover with a dry cloth. Set aside 45 minutes. Add remaining all-purpose flour, 1/2 cup at a time, until dough pulls away from side of bowl. Turn out on a lightly floured board. Knead dough, adding flour as needed, until smooth and elastic. Clean and grease bowl. Place dough in bowl, turning to grease all sides. Cover with a dry cloth. Let rise in a warm place until doubled in size, about 2 hours. Punch down dough by pushing your fist into center; pull edges of dough over center. Turn out dough on a lightly floured surface. Knead 5 times. Grease a baking sheet. Sprinkle generously with cornmeal. Roll out dough to a 16" x 10" rectangle. Tightly roll up rectangle, starting at the shorter side. Use your finger tips to pinch roll tight. Pinch seams together. Using the palms of your hands, press on the ends of loaf, rolling back and forth on work surface to taper ends. Place loaf, seam-side down, on greased baking sheet. Cover loaf with a dry cloth. Let rise until light, about 45 minutes. In a small saucepan, combine cornstarch and 1/2 cup cold water. Bring to a boil, stirring constantly. Cool until slightly warm. Preheat oven to 400F (205C). Fill a baking pan with boiling water to a depth of 1 inch. Place on lowest oven rack. Brush cornstarch mixture on loaf. With a razor blade or sharp knife, make 2 (1/2-inch-deep) diagonal slashes in loaf. Bake 10 minutes. Stir cornstarch mixture; brush on loaf again. Bake 20 minutes, brushing 2 more times, until golden brown and loaf sounds hollow when tapped with your fingers. Immediately remove from baking sheet. Cool on a rack. Makes 1 loaf.

Dilled Yogurt Sauce

Try tossing sauce with a chef-type salad and stuffing in pocket bread.

1/2 cup vegetable oil
1 egg yolk
2 tablespoons white-wine vinegar
1 tablespoon sugar

1/2 teaspoon salt
2 tablespoons Dijon-style mustard
1/2 cup plain yogurt
1 teaspoon dried dillweed

In a blender, combine oil, egg yolk, vinegar, sugar, salt and mustard. Process until smooth and thickened. Pour sauce into a bowl. Stir in yogurt and dillweed. Refrigerate 4 hours before serving. Store in an airtight container in refrigerator up to 1 week. Makes about 1 cup.

Honey-Wheat-Nugget Bread

Find cracked wheat at a health-food store or in the cereal section of the supermarket.

1/4 cup warm water (105F, 40C)	1/4 cup honey
1 (1/4-oz.) pkg. active dry yeast	2 tablespoons vegetable oil
(1 tablespoon)	1 teaspoon salt
1 teaspoon honey	1-1/2 cups whole-wheat flour
1 cup warm water (105F, 40C)	1-1/2 to 2 cups bread flour or
1/3 cup non-fat dry milk powder	all-purpose flour
1/2 cup cracked wheat	

Pour 1/4 cup warm water into a small bowl; stir in yeast and honey until dissolved. Set aside until foamy, about 15 minutes. In a large bowl, combine 1 cup warm water, milk powder and cracked wheat. Set aside 10 minutes. Stir in yeast mixture, 1/4 cup honey, oil and salt. Add whole-wheat flour; beat until smooth. Cover with a dry cloth. Set aside 20 minutes. Add bread flour or all-purpose flour, 1/2 cup at a time, until dough pulls away from side of bowl. Turn out on a lightly floured board. Knead dough, adding flour as needed, until smooth and elastic. Clean and grease bowl. Place dough in bowl, turning to grease all sides. Cover with a dry cloth. Let rise in a warm place until doubled in size, about 2 hours. Punch down dough by pushing your fist into center; pull edges of dough over center. Turn out dough on a lightly floured surface. Knead 5 times. Grease a 9" x 5" loaf pan. Shape dough into a loaf. Place in greased pan. Cover with a dry cloth. Let rise until light, about 45 minutes. Preheat oven to 375F (190C). Bake until golden brown and loaf sounds hollow when tapped with your fingers, 30 to 35 minutes. Immediately remove from pan. Cool on a rack. Makes 1 loaf.

Crunchy Granola Bread

A hint of fruity sweetness makes this so good with nut-butter spreads.

1/4 cup warm water (105F, 40C)	1 tablespoon vegetable oil
1 (1/4-oz.) pkg. active dry yeast	1 cup whole-wheat flour
(1 tablespoon)	1-1/2 to 2 cups bread flour or
1 teaspoon honey	all-purpose flour
1 cup apple juice	1-1/2 cups fruit and nut granola
1 teaspoon salt	

Pour 1/4 cup warm water into a small bowl; stir in yeast and honey until dissolved. Set aside until foamy, about 15 minutes. In a large bowl, combine apple juice, salt and oil. Add yeast mixture, whole-wheat flour and 1 cup bread flour or all-purpose flour; beat until smooth. Cover with a dry cloth. Set aside 20 minutes. Add 1-1/4 cups granola and remaining bread flour or all-purpose flour, 1/2 cup at a time, until dough pulls away from side of bowl. Turn out on a lightly floured board. Knead dough, adding flour as necessary, until smooth and elastic. Clean and grease bowl. Place dough in bowl, turning to grease all sides. Cover with a dry cloth. Let rise in a warm place until doubled in size, about 2 hours. Punch down dough by pushing your fist into center; pull edges of dough over center. Turn out dough on a lightly floured surface. Knead 5 times. Grease a 9" x 5" loaf pan. Shape dough into a loaf. Place loaf in greased pan. Sprinkle 1/4 cup granola over loaf; press into loaf. Cover with a dry cloth. Let rise until light, about 45 minutes. Preheat oven to 375F (190C). Bake until browned and loaf sounds hollow when tapped with your fingers, 30 to 35 minutes. Immediately remove from pan. Cool on a rack. Makes 1 loaf.

Sesame-Whole-Wheat Bread

A nutty-flavored bread, especially good for egg-salad or tuna-salad sandwiches.

1/2 cup warm water (105F, 40C)	2 teaspoons salt
1 teaspoon honey	2 cups bread flour or all-purpose flour
2 (1/4-oz.) pkgs. active dry yeast	4-1/2 to 5 cups whole-wheat flour
(2 tablespoons)	1 egg
2 cups milk	1/4 cup milk
1/4 cup packed brown sugar	1/4 cup sesame seeds
1/4 cup butter or margarine	

Pour 1/2 cup warm water into a small bowl; stir in honey and yeast until dissolved. Set aside until foamy, about 15 minutes. Heat 2 cups milk in a small saucepan until bubbles form around edge of pan; pour milk into a large bowl. Add brown sugar, butter or margarine and salt. Cool to 105F (40C) or until a few drops on your wrist feel warm. Stir in yeast mixture. Add 2 cups bread flour or all-purpose flour and 1 cup whole-wheat flour; beat until smooth. Cover with a dry cloth. Set aside 20 minutes. Add remaining whole-wheat flour, 1/2 cup at a time, until dough pulls away from side of bowl. Turn out on a lightly floured board. Knead dough, adding flour as necessary, until smooth and elastic. Clean and grease bowl. Place dough in bowl, turning to grease all sides. Cover with a dry cloth. Let rise in a warm place until doubled in size, about 2 hours. Punch down dough by pushing your fist into center; pull edges of dough over center. Turn out dough on a lightly floured surface. Knead 5 times. Divide dough in half. Grease 2 (9" x 5") loaf pans. Shape each dough half into a loaf. Place in greased pans. In a small bowl, beat egg with 1/4 cup milk; brush loaves with egg mixture. Sprinkle generously with sesame seeds; press seeds into dough. Cover with a dry cloth. Let rise until light, about 45 minutes. Preheat oven to 375F (190C). Bake until browned and loaves sound hollow when tapped with your fingers, 30 to 35 minutes. Immediately remove from pans. Cool on a rack. Makes 2 loaves.

Variations

Sesame-Whole-Wheat Buns: Prepare dough as above. Divide into 16 equal parts; shape each into a smooth ball. Place on a greased baking sheet 3 inches apart. Slightly flatten balls by rolling over them with a rolling pin; brush with egg mixture. Sprinkle generously with sesame seeds; press seeds into buns. Cover with a dry cloth. Let rise until light, about 30 minutes. Preheat oven to 375F (190C). Bake until golden brown, about 20 minutes. Immediately remove from baking sheets. Cool on a rack. Makes 16 buns.

Goliath Sesame-Seed Buns: Prepare dough as above. Divide into 2 parts; shape each into a smooth ball. Place on 2 greased baking sheets. Flatten balls into 10-inch circles with a rolling pin. Continue as for small buns but let rise 45 minutes. Bake until golden brown, about 30 minutes. Cool as above. Makes 2 buns.

If bread dough is difficult to handle, oil your hands lightly before kneading.

Herb Bread

Try making this bread with other herbs, like rosemary, or with a herb bouquet.

1/4 cup warm water (105F, 40C)
1 teaspoon sugar
1 (1/4-oz.) pkg. active dry yeast
   (1 tablespoon)
1 (8-oz.) carton plain yogurt (1 cup)
1/2 cup milk
1 teaspoon salt
1 tablespoon dried dillweed

2 tablespoons vegetable oil
1 egg, beaten
2 cups all-purpose flour
1-1/2 to 2 cups bread flour or
   all-purpose flour
1 teaspoon melted butter or margarine
2 tablespoons freshly grated Parmesan cheese

Pour 1/4 cup warm water into a small bowl; stir in sugar and yeast until dissolved. Set aside until foamy, about 15 minutes. In a small saucepan, stir together yogurt, milk, salt, dillweed and oil; heat until warm. Pour into a large bowl; stir in yeast mixture and egg. Add 2 cups all-purpose flour; beat until smooth. Cover with a dry cloth. Set aside 20 minutes. Add bread flour or all-purpose flour, 1/2 cup at a time, until dough pulls away from side of bowl. Turn out on a lightly floured board. Knead dough, adding flour as needed, until smooth and elastic. Clean and grease bowl. Place dough in bowl, turning to grease all sides. Cover with a dry cloth. Let rise in a warm place until doubled in size, about 2 hours. Punch down dough by pushing your fist into center; pull edges of dough over center. Turn out dough on a lightly floured surface. Knead 5 times. Divide dough in half. Grease a 9" x 5" loaf pan. Shape each dough half into a 12-inch rope. Twist ropes together 3 times. Press ends together and fold under. Place twisted loaf in greased pan. Cover with a dry cloth. Let rise until light, about 45 minutes. Preheat oven to 375F (190C). Bake 30 minutes. Brush with butter or margarine. Bake 5 to 10 minutes longer or until browned and loaf sounds hollow when tapped with your fingers. Immediately remove from pan. Sprinkle loaf with Parmesan cheese. Cool on a rack. Makes 1 loaf.

Tartar Sauce

Great for deep-fried-fish sandwiches. Try with chicken or turkey, too.

1/2 cup mayonnaise
1 tablespoon chopped sweet pickle or
   pickle relish
1 teaspoon grated onion

1 tablespoon finely chopped fresh parsley
1/2 teaspoon Worcestershire sauce
1-1/2 teaspoons chopped capers
White pepper to taste

In a small bowl, combine mayonnaise, pickle or pickle relish, onion, parsley, Worcestershire sauce and capers. Season to taste with white pepper. Store in an airtight container in refrigerator at least 30 minutes before using. Use within 2 or 3 days. Makes about 1/2 cup.

For Breakfast

oups and sandwiches offer a break in the routine of cold, ready-to-eat cereal or eggs, bacon and toast. Flavors that mean breakfast to most of us are experienced anew in the form of a soup like Bacon & Egg Chowder. Sandwiches allow us to have different tastes for breakfast, such as Seafood Eggs Benedict. Even breakfast-skippers can be enticed to sit down to a Waffled Bacon & Cheese Sandwich.

Soups and sandwiches for breakfast are novel and offer a change of pace. Packed with healthy ingredients, they far outweigh a sweet roll or toast and coffee for nutrition. For hurried workdays and school days, convenience is a must. Some breakfast soups and sandwiches take minutes to prepare, like Raisin-Custard Soup or Granola-Stripe Sandwiches. Others can be prepared the night before. Raspberry-Pineapple Wake-Up is ready to pour and enjoy straight from the refrigerator. In the morning, French Cheese Rolls are dipped in egg and browned in butter for a special send-off.

Soups and sandwiches make good hot or cold breakfasts. On cold blustery days, Raisin-Custard Soup will warm you. During the heat of summer, Orange-Banana Bisque is as refreshing as its name. Choose the soup or sandwich to fit your mood as well as the weather.

When time permits, use recipes with more involved preparations for a weekend brunch. Islands in the Sun is a combination soup and sandwich, ideal for entertaining or special family occasions. The crepe island is folded around a cheese, orange and pineapple filling. Orange-pineapple soup ladled around the islands in individual bowls creates a tempting dish. Crepes and soup can be prepared ahead so the only last-minute task is putting each serving together.

A soup or sandwich may need only a fruit or juice, toast or muffin to make a complete breakfast. Or, choose a soup and sandwich together, as shown in the menu below, for a perfect match. ❧

Menu

Hurried Monday on the Run
Raisin-Custard Soup, page 66
Sesame-Fruit Fingers, page 61
Hot Herbal Tea

Leisurely Sunday Brunch
Orange-Banana Bisque, page 65
Assorted Crackers
Seafood Eggs Benedict, page 58
Tomato & Avocado Slices
Coffee

Seafood Eggs Benedict

Quick Hollandaise Sauce can be stored in the refrigerator several days.

1 lb. fresh asparagus spears or
   1 (14-1/2-oz.) can asparagus spears,
   with liquid
1/2 lb. frozen cooked shrimp or crabmeat
2 cups boiling water
Quick Hollandaise Sauce, see below
8 slices English-Muffin Bread, page 51, or
   4 English muffins, split

3 tablespoons Savory Butter, page 36,
   butter or margarine, room temperature
4 extra-large eggs
1 tablespoon vinegar
Paprika
2 thin slices lemon, cut in half

Quick Hollandaise Sauce:
1/2 cup butter or margarine
3 egg yolks
2 tablespoons lemon juice

Salt to taste
Red (cayenne) pepper or white pepper

Wash fresh asparagus. Snap off heavy woody ends; discard. Cut into 2- to 3-inch spears. Cook asparagus in a saucepan in a small amount of water until barely tender, 10 to 15 minutes. If using canned asparagus, warm in a saucepan in aparagus liquid, 5 minutes. Keep asparagus warm. Heat shrimp in 2 cups boiling water 3 minutes. If using crabmeat, warm in a small saucepan with 2 tablespoons water. Keep shrimp or crabmeat warm. Prepare Quick Hollandaise Sauce. Keep warm in a double boiler or small saucepan over hot but not boiling water. Toast bread slices or English muffins. Spread with Savory Butter, butter or margarine. Poach eggs in an egg poacher or as follows: Bring water, 1 inch deep, to a simmer with vinegar in a large skillet. Break 1 egg into a small bowl. Slip egg from bowl into simmering water. Repeat with remaining eggs. Cook over low heat until whites are firm, 3 to 5 minutes. Do not allow water to boil. Remove eggs with a slotted spoon. Trim edges neatly. For each serving, cut 2 bread slices or 1 split English muffin in half. Arrange 4 halves on each plate in a wheel with 1 corner of each half touching. Place asparagus spears and shrimp or crabmeat on each muffin. Place 1 poached egg in the center of each wheel. Spoon warm Hollandaise Sauce over eggs. Sprinkle paprika over top. Twist 1 half lemon slice and stand it, peel-side up, on top of each egg. Makes 4 servings.

Quick Hollandaise Sauce:
Melt butter or margarine in a small saucepan. Pour clear liquid from melted butter or margarine into a small bowl. Discard white solids remaining in pan. Combine egg yolks and lemon juice in a blender. Switch on and off to mix well. With blender on medium-high speed, pour melted butter or margarine in a steady stream into yolk mixture. Process until all butter or margarine has been added. Season to taste with salt and red pepper or white pepper.

Variation

Seafood Eggs Benedict for a Crowd: Double or triple recipe. Prepare poached eggs as above the day before. Place cooked eggs in water to cover in a casserole with a lid. Store in refrigerator. One hour before serving, drain eggs. Set aside to come to room temperature. Pour boiling water around eggs. Cover and let stand 5 minutes. Drain eggs, and continue putting sandwiches together.

How to Make Seafood Eggs Benedict

1/Arrange bread on plates in a wheel pattern. Place asparagus spears and shrimp or crabmeat on bread.

2/Place poached egg in center of wheel arrangement. Spoon or pour warm Hollandaise Sauce over egg.

Raspberry-Pineapple Wake-Up

Prepare the night before or chill ingredients for a breakfast on the run.

2 slices Sesame-Whole-Wheat Bread,
   page 55, or other firm-textured
   whole-wheat bread
2 tablespoons butter or margarine
1/4 cup sliced almonds
1 teaspoon brown sugar
2 eggs

2 (8-oz.) cartons raspberry-flavored yogurt
   (2 cups)
2 cups milk
1 (8-oz.) can juice-packed crushed pineapple
1 tablespoon lemon juice
1/4 teaspoon ground cinnamon

Break bread in pieces; place in a blender or food processor. Process to medium crumbs. Melt butter or margarine in a small skillet over medium heat. Toss breadcrumbs in skillet. Add almonds; stir until crumbs are golden brown. Remove from heat. Sprinkle brown sugar over crumb mixture; stir. Cool crumb mixture to room temperature. Beat eggs in a medium bowl until light and airy. Stir yogurt in cartons to combine fruit and yogurt. Add yogurt to eggs; beat until smooth. Stir in milk, pineapple with juice, lemon juice and cinnamon. Cover and refrigerate overnight or until ready to serve. To serve, ladle cold soup into individual bowls. Sprinkle with breadcrumb mixture. Makes 4 (1-1/4-cup) servings.

Battered Corners

With a variety of fillings, these hot puffy sandwiches will become a favorite at your house.

6 slices Home-Style White Bread, page 33,
   or other white bread
1/2 (5-oz.) jar sharp-cheese spread
6 crisp-cooked bacon slices, crumbled
2 cups all-purpose flour
1 tablespoon baking powder

1 teaspoon salt
1 egg
1-1/2 cups buttermilk
1/3 cup shortening, melted
Oil for deep-frying

Cut crust from bread. Spread 3 slices generously with cheese spread. Sprinkle crumbled bacon over cheese-spread slices. Top with remaining 3 slices bread. Cut each sandwich, corner to corner, into 4 triangles; set aside. Sift together flour, baking powder and salt into a medium bowl. Beat egg in another medium bowl until frothy. Stir buttermilk and shortening into egg. Add egg mixture to flour mixture, beating until smooth. Pour oil in a heavy skillet or deep-fryer to 2-inch depth. Heat oil to 350F (175C) or until a 1-inch cube of bread added to oil turns brown in 60 seconds. Dip sandwiches in batter; turn to cover completely. Fry sandwiches until golden brown, about 1 minute on each side. Drain on paper towels. Serve warm. Makes 12 sandwiches or 6 servings.

Variations

Peanut-Butter-Banana Battered Corners: Spread 3 slices bread with peanut butter. Thinly slice 2 medium bananas over bread. Drizzle bananas with honey. Top with remaining 3 slices bread. Press to prevent banana from falling out. Cut, corner to corner, into 4 triangles. Prepare batter and fry corners as above.

Cheese & Jelly Battered Corners: Beat 1 (3-ounce) package cream cheese and 1 tablespoon milk until smooth. Spread on 3 slices bread. Spread 1 tablespoon of your favorite jelly or jam on each slice. Top with remaining 3 slices bread. Cut, corner to corner, into 4 triangles. Prepare batter and fry corners as above.

Ham & Pineapple Battered Corners: Drain 1 (8-ounce) can crushed pineapple, pressing to remove all the juice. Place 1 slice sandwich ham on each of 3 slices bread. Spoon pineapple over ham. Top with remaining 3 slices bread. Press to prevent pineapple from falling out. Cut, corner to corner, into 4 triangles. Prepare batter and fry corners as above.

Cream-Cheese & Lox Battered Corners: Beat 1 (3-ounce) package cream cheese and 1 tablespoon milk until smooth. Spread on 3 slices bread. Layer 2 strips lox over each. Top with remaining 3 slices bread. Cut, corner to corner, into 4 triangles. Prepare batter and fry corners as above.

Battered Corners with Chocolate Pieces: Beat 1 (3-ounce) package cream cheese with 1 tablespoon milk and 2 tablespoons powdered sugar until light. Stir in 1/3 cup semisweet or milk chocolate pieces. Spread 3 slices bread with chocolate mixture. Top with remaining 3 slices bread. Cut, corner to corner, into 4 triangles. Prepare batter and fry corners as above.

Waffled Bacon & Cheese Sandwiches

A waffle iron makes an interesting pattern on this toasted treat.

8 slices Home-Style White Bread, page 33,
   or other white bread
1/4 cup butter or margarine,
   room temperature

1/4 cup apple butter
4 oz. sliced Canadian bacon or sandwich ham
4 (1-oz.) slices American cheese
Orange slices, if desired

Preheat waffle iron as manufacturer directs. Spread 1 side of 4 slices of bread with about 1/3 of the butter or margarine. Place slices, buttered-side down, on a sheet of waxed paper. Spread about 1 tablespoon apple butter over bread. Place Canadian bacon or ham and cheese on top. Spread both sides of remaining 4 slices bread with remaining butter or margarine. Place on top of sandwiches. Place sandwiches in hot waffle iron; close waffle iron. Heat until cheese melts and sandwich is golden brown, 2 to 3 minutes. Cut sandwiches in half, corner to corner. Top with overlapping orange slices, if desired. Makes 4 servings.

Variation

Waffled Ham & Pineapple Sandwiches: Omit apple butter. Spread 2 tablespoons well-drained crushed pineapple over 4 slices bread. Substitute 4 ounces sliced Monterey Jack cheese for American cheese. Layer ham or Canadian bacon and cheese on pineapple. Assemble and cook as above.

Sesame-Fruit Fingers

Use Fruit-Nut Bread made with prunes or raisins for a flavorful coffeetime sandwich.

1/2 loaf Fruit-Nut Bread, page 37, or
   10 slices other raisin-nut bread
1 (3-oz.) pkg. cream cheese,
   room temperature

1 tablespoon milk
1/3 cup orange marmalade
1/3 cup Sesame-Nut Butter, page 37,
   room temperature

If preparing Fruit-Nut Bread, cool 8 hours or overnight. Cut 10 slices of Fruit-Nut Bread, about 1/4 inch thick. In a small bowl, beat cream cheese and milk with an electric mixer until smooth. Spread cream-cheese mixture on 5 bread slices. Spread marmalade over cheese mixture. Spread remaining slices with Sesame-Nut Butter. Place on top of marmalade-spread slices, nut-buttered-side down. Cut each sandwich in 1-inch-wide fingers. Makes about 20 finger sandwiches or 5 servings.

Storing nut butters in the refrigerator helps prevent separation. If oil separates, stir butter before using.

Cheese Croissants à l'Orange

Easy to prepare for a leisurely breakfast.

2 tablespoons butter or margarine
2 tablespoons sugar
1-1/2 teaspoons cornstarch
1/2 cup orange juice
1 cup ricotta cheese (8 oz.)

1 (8-oz.) carton orange-flavored yogurt
   (1 cup)
1 (11-oz.) can mandarin-orange sections,
   drained
4 Croissants, page 44, or other croissants

In a small saucepan, melt butter or margarine. Stir sugar and cornstarch into orange juice until dissolved. Add to melted butter or margarine. Cook over medium heat, stirring constantly, until thickened and translucent. Remove from heat and cover. Cool slightly. In a small bowl, stir together cheese and yogurt until smooth. Fold in orange sections. Split croissants horizontally. Spoon about 1/2 cup cheese mixture on bottom of each croissant. Place top of roll on filling. Spoon about 2 tablespoons orange sauce over each croissant. Serve immediately. Makes 4 servings.

Bacon & Egg Chowder

Familiar breakfast fare served in an unfamiliar way.

3 tablespoons butter or margarine
6 tablespoons all-purpose flour
1 teaspoon Dijon-style mustard
1 cup Chicken Broth, page 16, or
   canned regular-strength chicken broth
3 cups milk
1/2 teaspoon salt

1/2 teaspoon Worcestershire sauce
3 hard-cooked eggs
6 crisp-cooked bacon slices, crumbled
2 tablespoons vegetable oil
1-1/2 cups frozen Southern-style
   hash-brown potatoes

Melt butter or margarine in a 3-quart saucepan. Add flour and mustard; stir until smooth. Remove from heat. Add a small amount of broth, stirring constantly until a smooth paste forms. Stir in remaining broth and milk. Bring to a boil over medium-high heat, stirring constantly. Season with salt and Worcestershire sauce. Cut hard-cooked eggs in half. Remove egg yolks; set aside. Cut egg whites in 1/2-inch cubes. Add egg whites and bacon to broth mixture. Keep broth mixture warm, but do not boil. Heat oil in a large skillet. Add potatoes. Cook over medium-low heat, turning potatoes occasionally, until tender and browned, about 10 minutes. Add browned potatoes to chowder. Ladle hot chowder into individual bowls. Force egg yolks through a fine sieve. Top each serving with sieved egg yolk. Makes 4 (1-1/2 cup) servings.

Granola-Stripe Sandwiches

Children will be especially delighted with the banana and granola stripes.

4 slices Scots Oat Bread, page 46, or
    other oatmeal or whole-wheat bread
3 tablespoons butter or margarine,
    room temperature
6 tablespoons peanut butter

2 small bananas, sliced
2 tablespoons honey
3/4 cup granola

Spread bread slices with butter or margarine. Generously spread peanut butter on bread. Arrange diagonal rows of banana slices on top. Drizzle stripes of honey between rows of banana. Pile granola on honey stripes. Cut sandwiches diagonally along 1 stripe. Serve immediately. Makes 4 servings.

How to Make Granola-Stripe Sandwiches

1/Spread peanut butter on bread. Arrange diagonal rows of banana slices on bread.

2/Drizzle stripes of honey between rows of banana. Pile granola on honey stripes.

Islands in the Sun

Tropical-fruit-filled crepes floating in a sunny soup.

6 Crepes, see below
1 cup creamed cottage cheese (8 oz.)
1 (11-oz.) can mandarin-orange sections,
   drained
1 (8-oz.) can crushed pineapple, drained

Ground nutmeg to taste
1/4 cup cornstarch
1/3 cup sugar
1 (48-oz.) can orange-pineapple juice
1/4 cup sliced almonds

Crepes:
1 egg
1/2 cup milk
1/2 cup all-purpose flour

1 tablespoon butter or margarine, melted
Butter or margarine

Prepare Crepes. In a small saucepan, combine cottage cheese, orange sections and pineapple. Season with nutmeg to taste. Heat over low heat, stirring occasionally, until barely warm; set aside. In a 3-quart saucepan, combine cornstarch and sugar; stir until combined. Add orange-pineapple juice. Stir over medium heat until mixture thickens and comes to a boil; keep warm. To serve, place a warm crepe flat on a board or plate. Spoon about 1/3 cup fruit-cheese mixture on center of crepe. Fold 2 sides over filling, overlapping sides slightly. Fold 1 end over filling. Roll crepe to other end. Place crepe, folded-side down, in an individual bowl. Repeat with remaining crepes and filling. Ladle hot soup around filled crepe in each bowl. Sprinkle almonds over top. Makes 6 servings.

Crepes:
Combine egg, milk and flour in a blender; process 1 minute. Scrape down sides of container. Add melted butter or margarine; process 1 minute longer. Refrigerate batter at least 1 hour or overnight. Melt 1 teaspoon butter or margarine in 9-inch crepe pan or small skillet. Heat until bubbly. With 1 hand, pour 2 tablespoons batter in pan. At the same time, lift pan off burner and tilt in all directions. Batter should cover bottom of pan with a thin layer. If necessary, add a small amount of batter to fill in bare spots. Return pan to medium-high heat. Cook until lightly browned, about 2 minutes. Turn crepe and brown other side a few seconds. Remove from pan. Repeat with remaining batter, adding butter or margarine to skillet as necessary. Stack cooked crepes on a plate. Place in a warm oven, if desired.

Orange-Banana Bisque

Greet guests for brunch with stemmed glasses of chilled soup.

Almond Crunch, page 27
1 cup orange juice
2 cups milk

1 cup half and half
1 tablespoon lemon juice
4 bananas, sliced

Prepare Almond Crunch. Combine orange juice, milk, half and half, lemon juice and bananas in a blender or food processor. Process until smooth. Pour juice mixture into an airtight container. Chill thoroughly, 2 to 4 hours. Serve in chilled, stemmed sherbet glasses. Top each serving with Almond Crunch. Makes 4 (1-1/4 cup) servings.

Raisin-Custard Soup

Delicious served either warm or cold.

Almond Crunch, page 27, if desired
1 qt. milk (4 cups)
1/2 cup raisins
1/2 cup sugar
1/4 teaspoon salt

2 tablespoons cornstarch
2 eggs
1 cup cooked rice
1 teaspoon vanilla extract

Prepare Almond Crunch, if desired. Scald milk by heating in a large saucepan over low heat until bubbles appear around the edge. Place raisins in a medium bowl. Pour hot milk over raisins. Let stand 15 minutes. Combine sugar, salt and cornstarch in a 3-quart saucepan. Add eggs. Gradually stir warm milk mixture into egg mixture. Cook over medium heat, stirring constantly, until thickened. Do not boil. Remove from heat. Stir in cooked rice and vanilla. Cool until only slightly warm, or refrigerate in an airtight container until well chilled, 3 hours or more. Serve warm or cold. Top each serving with Almond Crunch, if desired. Makes 4 (1-cup) servings.

French Cheese Rolls

As fancy as crepes, but so simple!

1 (3-oz.) pkg. cream cheese,
   room temperature
1 tablespoon milk
8 slices soft white bread
1/2 cup strawberry or raspberry preserves
2 eggs

1/4 cup milk
1/4 teaspoon salt
1 tablespoon butter or margarine
Sliced fresh strawberries, if desired
Powdered sugar

In a small bowl, beat cream cheese with an electric mixer until soft. Add milk; continue beating until smooth. Cut crust from bread. Roll over each slice once with rolling pin to flatten slightly. Spread each bread slice with cream-cheese mixture and 1 tablespoon preserves. Roll up each slice, jelly-roll fashion. Wrap rolls individually in waxed paper or plastic wrap. Refrigerate overnight or at least 2 hours. Place eggs, milk and salt in a pie plate or cake pan. Beat with a fork or whisk until just combined. Melt butter or margarine in a large skillet. Dip each roll in egg mixture, coating all sides. Fry in hot butter or margarine until browned all over. Drain on paper towels. Place 2 rolls on each plate. Arrange strawberry slices on rolls, if desired. Sift powdered sugar over the top. Makes 4 servings.

Appetizers

Appetizers are usually reserved for guests and holiday family meals. Tasty morsels are served as the introduction or first course to a special meal. These tidbits should be light and stimulating to the taste buds without competing with the food that will follow. Gatherings of friends anytime of day for any reason call for a little something to eat. Soups and sandwiches fit the situation. They are the ideal solution for the first course to a formal dinner or a tasty tidbit served by itself.

Soups can be light yet have an arousing flavor, like Creamy Beet Swirl. Other soups, such as Asparagus Vichyssoise or Watercress Soup, are rich and filling and should be served in small portions.

Appetizer sandwiches are bite-size and easy to eat for formal and informal occasions. Open-face appetizer sandwiches are often called *canapés*. The word in French literally means *couch*. When referring to sandwiches, canapés are dainty pieces of bread, cracker or pastry with a savory topping sitting on it as if on a couch. Used as appetizers for a buffet or a snack at a cocktail party, Egg & Pâté Checkerboards, Spinach-Cheese Squares and Garlic-Shrimp Rounds make up an attractive tray. For quick-to-make canapés, cut any firm-textured bread into small squares, circles or different shapes. Top with a bread spread like Caraway-Cheese Spread, Chili-Avocado Spread or Fruit & Nut Butter.

Soups and sandwiches make easy appetizers because most can be prepared ahead. Chilled soups such as Iced Crab-Avocado Soup or Champagne Consommé need no last-minute fussing. Chili-con-Queso Pinwheels or Spinach-Cheese Squares can be made hours before guests arrive. Pop them in the oven when the door bell rings. Fresh, hot sandwich bites will be ready to serve in minutes.

Menu

Progressive-Dinner Opener

Iced Crab-Avocado Soup, page 73
Cracker Balls, page 23
Ham & Cheese Devils, page 69
Monte Cristo Bites, page 76
Spinach-Cheese Squares, page 68
Wine Spritzers

Sweetheart Dinner for Two

Champagne Consommé, page 75
Cheese Pretzels, page 22
Roast Game Hens with Wild-Rice Stuffing
& Chutney Glaze
French Green Beans & Slivered Brazil Nuts
Fresh Spinach, Tomato Wedges
& Mushroom Salad
Strawberry Ribbons, page 154

Spinach-Cheese Squares

Buy filo or strudel dough in the frozen-food section of your supermarket.

1 tablespoon butter or margarine
2 green onions including 2 inches of
   green tops, sliced
1 tablespoon chopped fresh parsley
1/4 teaspoon dried dillweed
2 cups packed fresh spinach leaves, shredded

2 oz. feta cheese, crumbled
1 egg, beaten
1/4 cup butter or margarine, melted
2 tablespoons olive oil
8 sheets filo or strudel dough, thawed

Melt 1 tablespoon butter or margarine in a medium saucepan. Add green onions; sauté 1 minute. Add parsley, dillweed and spinach; stir. Cover and cook over low heat until spinach is wilted and tender, 3 to 5 minutes. Drain spinach mixture, using a fine sieve and pressing to release all liquid. In a small bowl, combine drained spinach mixture, cheese and egg. Combine 1/4 cup melted butter or margarine and olive oil in a small bowl. Spread 1 sheet filo or strudel dough on a flat surface. Keep remaining sheets covered with plastic wrap or a barely damp cloth. Brush sheet with butter-oil mixture. Fold in half crosswise; brush again. Cut sheet into 3-inch crosswise strips. Place about 2 teaspoons spinach filling 1/3 the distance from 1 end of each strip. Fold shorter end over filling. Fold long sides of strip over filling. Turn filling over and over to end of strip, forming a square package. Brush tops with butter-oil mixture. Repeat with remaining dough sheets and filling. Squares may be refrigerated, tightly covered, until needed or overnight. Preheat oven to 400F (205C). Lightly grease a baking sheet. Place squares on greased baking sheet, 1 inch apart. Bake until lightly browned, 15 to 20 minutes. Serve warm or at room temperature. Makes 32 appetizer servings.

Watercresss Soup

Watercress has a distinctive, peppery flavor.

3 leeks, white part only
1 medium potato, peeled, sliced
5 cups Chicken Broth, page 16, or
   3 (14-1/2-oz.) cans regular-
   strength chicken broth
1/2 teaspoon salt

1/4 teaspoon white pepper
2 cups watercress leaves and stems
1 (3-oz.) pkg. cream cheese,
   room temperature
Freshly grated or ground nutmeg, if desired

Wash leeks thoroughly. Trim and slice. In a 4-quart pot, combine leeks, potato slices, broth, salt and white pepper. Cover and simmer until potato is tender, 20 to 25 minutes. Add watercress; simmer 5 minutes longer. Press leek mixture through a food mill or sieve. Or puree in a blender or food processor and strain through a fine sieve. Return mixture to pot. Beat cream cheese with an electric mixer until smooth. Add about 1/2 cup soup mixture to cheese. Beat again until smooth. Add cream-cheese mixture to soup. Stir over medium heat until cheese melts. Ladle hot soup into individual bowls. Top each serving with a sprinkling of nutmeg, if desired. Makes 6 (1-cup) servings.

How to Make Spinach-Cheese Squares

1/Fold buttered sheets in half. Cut into 3-inch-wide strips. Spoon about 2 teaspoons spinach filling 1/3 the distance from 1 end of each strip.

2/Fold shorter end over filling. Fold long sides of strip over filling. Turn filling over and over to end of strip, forming square package. Brush with butter-oil mixture.

Ham & Cheese Devils

Hot-pepper jelly or jalapeño jelly can be found in specialty-food stores.

1/2 (3-oz.) pkg. cream cheese,
  room temperature
1 tablespoon mayonnaise
2 teaspoons Dijon-style mustard

1 (6-3/4-oz.) can chunk ham, chopped
8 slices Cheddar-Cheese Bread, page 38, or
  Italian bread
1/3 cup hot-pepper jelly

In a small bowl, beat cream cheese, mayonnaise and mustard with an electric mixer until smooth. Stir in ham. Toast bread. Use a round 1-1/2-inch cutter or small glass to cut toast into 32 (1-1/2-inch) circles. Using a nickel as a guide, cut a center circle from 16 of the toast rounds. Spread ham filling generously on remaining 16 rounds. Cover filling with rounds that have a center hole. Press edges together. Place a small spoonful of jelly in the center hole. Serve immediately. Makes 16 appetizer servings.

Egg & Pâté Checkerboards

Checkerboard filling keeps in the refrigerator several days.

1/2 lb. liverwurst, cut in 1-inch pieces
1 tablespoon dry sherry
2 tablespoons butter, room temperature
1 tablespoon chopped onion
Red (cayenne) pepper
4 hard-cooked eggs
1 teaspoon snipped fresh chives

1/8 teaspoon salt
1/8 teaspoon dry mustard
2 tablespoons mayonnaise
20 to 24 slices cocktail rye bread
8 French cornichons or small gherkins,
   thinly sliced diagonally

In a blender or food processor, combine liverwurst, sherry, butter and onion; process until smooth. Season to taste with red pepper. Refrigerate 2 hours. Press hard-cooked eggs through a sieve, using the back of a spoon. In a small bowl, combine sieved eggs, chives, salt, mustard and mayonnaise; refrigerate 2 hours. Place liverwurst mixture in a strip on a sheet of waxed paper. Roll it in the paper, forming a log the diameter of cocktail rye bread; refrigerate 1 hour. Place egg mixture in a strip on a sheet of waxed paper. Roll in paper, forming a log the same diameter as liver mixture; refrigerate 1 hour. Cut each log in half lengthwise. Cut each half again lengthwise, forming wedges. Place together 1 egg wedge and 1 pâté wedge, forming a half log. Repeat with remaining wedges. Place 2 half-logs together so that egg and pâté wedges alternate. Repeat with remaining half logs. Gently press logs together. Roll in waxed paper, keeping log shape. Refrigerate until ready to serve, up to 3 days. To serve, cut checkerboard in 1/2-inch-thick slices. Place on cocktail rye bread. Arrange 2 or 3 pickle slices on each checkerboard. Makes 20 to 24 appetizer servings.

Garlic-Shrimp Rounds

Shrimp are sized by the number per pound. Jumbo are 21 to 25 per pound.

10 raw jumbo shrimp (about 8 oz.)
1/3 cup olive oil or vegetable oil
1/3 cup dry white wine
2 garlic cloves, minced
2 tablespoons chopped fresh parsley
5 slices Herb Bread, page 56, or
   other white bread

2 tablespoons Lemon-Pepper Butter,
   page 41, room temperature
1/2 cup seafood-cocktail sauce
20 pickled cocktail onions

Peel, cut in half lengthwise and devein shrimp. Rinse under running cold water. Drain shrimp on paper towels. In a glass pie plate or casserole, combine oil, wine, garlic and parsley. Add shrimp; toss to coat shrimp completely. Marinate in refrigerator 4 hours or overnight. Preheat broiler. Use a round 1-1/2-inch cutter or small glass to cut rounds of bread. Spread bread rounds with Lemon-Pepper Butter. Arrange bread rounds on a baking sheet. Toast under broiler until lightly browned and crisp. Lift shrimp from marinade. Cook and stir in a skillet over medium heat until shrimp turn pink, 3 to 5 minutes, adding 1 to 2 tablespoons marinade, if necessary. Let shrimp cool slightly. Spoon 1 teaspoon seafood-cocktail sauce in the middle of each toasted bread round. Press 1 shrimp half into sauce. Arrange 1 pickled onion in the curl of the shrimp. Makes 20 appetizer servings.

How to Make Egg & Pâté Checkerboards

1/Cut egg and pâté logs in half lengthwise. Cut each half again lengthwise, forming wedges.

2/Put logs back together, alternating 2 egg wedges with 2 pâté wedges. To serve, cut in 1/2-inch-thick slices. Place on cocktail rye bread. Garnish with pickle slices.

Chili-con-Queso Pinwheels

So simple, this could be a spur-of-the-moment appetizer.

1 (8-oz.) can refrigerated crescent rolls
1 cup shredded Cheddar cheese (4 oz.)
1/3 cup canned diced green chilies

1/2 cup crushed nacho-cheese tortilla chips (about 20 chips)

Preheat oven to 375F (190C). Separate roll dough into 4 rectangles. Pinch together perforations. Sprinkle 1/4 cup cheese and 1 heaping tablespoon chilies over each rectangle. Roll up rectangles, jelly-roll fashion, from long side. Spread crushed chips on waxed paper. Roll dough logs in chips to coat outsides. Cut each log into 5 slices. Place slices, cut-side down, on an ungreased baking sheet. Bake until lightly browned, 15 to 20 minutes. Serve warm or at room temperature. Makes 20 appetizer servings.

Creamy Beet Swirl

A delicate pink color and a hint of orange make this cool soup a hit.

1 (16-oz.) can diced beets
1 tablespoon butter or margarine
1/4 cup chopped onion
1/2 teaspoon salt

Pinch ground cloves
1 cup dairy sour cream
1/2 cup orange juice
1 teaspoon cornstarch

Measure 1/3 cup beets with liquid from can to cover; set aside. Melt butter or margarine in a small skillet. Add onion; sauté until tender. In a blender or food processor, puree remaining beets and liquid, sautéed onion, salt, cloves, sour cream and 1/4 cup orange juice. Pour pureed mixture into an airtight container or casserole with a lid. Cover and refrigerate at least 4 hours or overnight. Finely chop 1/3 cup beets. Combine beets and liquid, remaining 1/4 cup orange juice and cornstarch in a small saucepan. Bring to a boil over medium heat, stirring constantly. Remove from heat; cool to room temperature. Refrigerate until ready to serve. To serve, pour chilled soup into a glass bowl. Pour thickened beet mixture over top of soup. Swirl through soup with a spoon. Makes 4 (3/4-cup) servings.

Artichoke Soup

Fresh artichokes add a more intense flavor to the frozen artichoke hearts.

2 fresh artichokes
1 (9-oz.) pkg. frozen artichoke hearts
1 qt. Chicken Broth, page 16, or
   2 (14-1/2-oz.) cans regular-
   strength chicken broth
1 tablespoon lemon juice
2 tablespoons butter or margarine

2 tablespoons minced shallots
1/4 cup all-purpose flour
1 cup whipping cream
3/4 teaspoon salt
1/8 teaspoon white pepper
1 tablespoon dry sherry
1/4 cup chopped roasted filberts

Trim stems of fresh artichokes even with base. Using kitchen shears, cut off tip of each leaf. Bring 6 cups water to a boil in a 4-quart pot. Add artichokes; boil until artichoke base is tender when pierced with a fork, about 45 minutes. Remove artichokes. Pull off heavy leaves; set aside. Remove and discard thin yellow and purple inner leaves and fuzzy choke from each artichoke. What remains is the *artichoke bottom*. Using a spoon, gently scrape tender pulp from heavy leaves. In a 4-quart pot, combine pulp, cleaned artichoke bottoms, frozen artichoke hearts, broth and lemon juice. Simmer 15 minutes. Place artichoke mixture in a blender or food processor; puree. Strain puree through a fine sieve. Rinse and dry pot. Melt butter or margarine in pot. Add shallots; sauté 1 minute. Stir in flour until blended. Gradually stir in artichoke puree. Bring to a boil, stirring constantly. Pour cream into a medium bowl. Slowly ladle about 1/2 cup hot artichoke mixture into cream; stir to blend. Pour cream mixture into artichoke mixture, stirring constantly. Add salt, pepper and sherry. Warm soup until heated through, stirring occasionally. Do not boil. Ladle hot soup into individual bowls. Sprinkle some chopped filberts over each serving. Makes 8 (1-cup) servings.

Iced Crab-Avocado Soup

Keeps its bright-green color even when stored overnight.

2 medium avocados
1 tablespoon lemon juice
2 tablespoons canned diced green chilies
2 tablespoons chopped onion
2 cups Chicken Broth, page 16, or
   1 (14-1/2-oz.) can regular-strength
   chicken broth

1 cup half and half
1/2 teaspoon salt
1 (6-oz.) pkg. frozen crabmeat, thawed
1 tablespoon chopped chives, if desired

Peel avocados. Cut flesh in 1-inch cubes. In a blender or food processor, puree avocado cubes, lemon juice, green chilies, onion and broth. Pour avocado mixture into a bowl or airtight container. Stir in half and half, salt and crabmeat. Cover and refrigerate until ready to serve. Ladle cold soup into chilled bowls or cups. Sprinkle with chives, if desired. Makes 6 (3/4-cup) servings.

Tart & Spicy Apple Soup

Serve as an introduction to roast pork or stuffed pork chops.

3 medium, tart green apples
2 tablespoons butter or margarine
1 cup chopped onion
1/2 teaspoon curry powder
1/4 teaspoon paprika
1/4 teaspoon salt
1/2 teaspoon grated lemon peel
3-1/2 cups Meat Broth, page 13; or
   1 (14-1/2-oz.) can regular-strength
   chicken broth and 1 (14-1/2-oz.) can
   regular-strength beef broth

1-1/2 tablespoons cornstarch
1/4 cup cold water
1 (8-oz.) carton plain yogurt (1 cup)
Sliced almonds, if desired

Cut 1 apple in half; set aside 1 half for garnish. Peel, core and slice remaining apples. Melt butter or margarine in a 3-quart saucepan. Add apple slices and onion; sauté until onion is tender. Add curry powder, paprika, salt, lemon peel and Meat Broth or canned broths. Bring to a boil; reduce heat. Cover and simmer 20 minutes. Pour mixture into a blender or food processor; puree. Or, force soup through a food mill or sieve. Return soup to saucepan. In a small bowl, stir cornstarch into cold water. Slowly pour cornstarch mixture into soup, stirring constantly. Cook over medium heat, stirring until thickened. Combine about 1/2 cup hot soup and yogurt in a small bowl; stir until smooth. Gradually stir yogurt mixture into remaining soup. Core reserved apple half; slice apple thinly. Ladle hot soup into individual bowls. Garnish each serving with several apple slices and sprinkle with almonds, if desired. Makes 6 (1-cup) servings.

Champagne Consommé

A delicate taste of elegance for a special chicken or seafood dinner.

3-1/2 cups Chicken Broth, page 16, or
   2 (14-1/2-oz.) cans regular-strength
   chicken broth
1/8 teaspoon dried leaf basil
1 egg white, slightly beaten
2 cups dry champagne
1/8 teaspoon Angostura bitters

2 (.25-oz.) envelopes unflavored gelatin
1/3 cup cold water
1/4 cup thin strips of cooked chicken or ham
1 cup seedless green grapes
6 medium shrimp, shelled, cooked
Parsley sprigs
Crackers, if desired

Combine broth, basil and egg white in a medium saucepan. Over medium heat, bring barely to a simmer, without stirring. Do not boil. Allow broth barely to simmer, 10 minutes. Do not stir. Remove from heat. Allow to cool, undisturbed, 10 minutes. Line a sieve with cheesecloth. Strain broth through sieve into a medium bowl. Return broth to saucepan. Add champagne and bitters. Bring to a boil. Stir gelatin into cold water. Add gelatin mixture to hot broth. Stir to dissolve. Remove from heat. Pour into a medium bowl or covered container. Refrigerate until slightly thickened, about 1 hour. Fold in chicken or ham strips and grapes. Refrigerate until consommé forms a soft gel, about 2 hours. Spoon into stemmed glasses. Garnish each serving with a cooked shrimp and a parsley sprig. Serve with crackers, if desired. Makes 6 (3/4-cup) servings.

Asparagus Vichyssoise

Classic vichyssoise is a rich potato-and-cream soup. Serve this variation hot or cold.

1 lb. fresh asparagus spears or 2 (10-oz.)
   pkgs. frozen asparagus spears
1/2 cup water
2 tablespoons butter or margarine
1/2 cup chopped onion
2 medium potatoes, peeled, sliced
2 cups Chicken Broth, page 16, or
   1 (14-1/2-oz.) can regular-
   strength chicken broth

1-1/2 cups water
1 teaspoon salt
1 egg
1/2 cup half and half

Wash fresh asparagus. Snap off heavy woody ends; discard. Cut off 6 fresh asparagus tips, about 1 inch long, to use as garnish. Cook fresh asparagus, including reserved tips, in 1/2 cup water until tender, about 10 minutes. Drain, discarding water. If using frozen asparagus, cook 5 minutes. Set aside 6 cooked tips for garnish. In a 3-quart saucepan, melt butter or margarine. Add onion; sauté until tender. Add potato slices, broth, 1-1/2 cups water and salt. Bring to a boil. Cover and simmer until potatoes are soft. In a blender or food processor, puree potato mixture and cooked asparagus. Pour pureed mixture through a sieve back into saucepan. Combine egg and half and half in a small bowl; beat well. Slowly pour egg mixture into pureed mixture, stirring constantly. Cook over low heat 5 minutes, stirring constantly. Do not boil. Serve soup hot, or refrigerate in an airtight container until thoroughly chilled, at least 4 hours. Ladle soup into shallow bowls. Float an asparagus tip in each bowl. Makes 6 (1-cup) servings.

Champagne Consommé

Monte Cristo Bites

May be prepared in advance to fry just before serving.

4 slices Home-Style White Bread, page 33, or other white bread	1 egg
3 oz. sliced ham	2 tablespoons milk
4 oz. sliced Gruyère or Swiss cheese	1/2 cup fresh breadcrumbs
3 oz. sliced cooked white meat of turkey or chicken	2 tablespoons freshly grated Parmesan cheese
	2 tablespoons butter or margarine
	2 tablespoons vegetable oil

Stack bread slices; trim crust, making straight sides. Place 1 bread slice on a board. Cover with half the ham and 1/3 of the cheese. Place another bread slice on top. Cover with half the turkey, 1/3 of the cheese and remaining ham, in layers. Top with another slice of bread. Cover with remaining turkey and cheese. Place remaining bread slice on top. Cut sandwich in 1-inch strips. Cut each strip in 1-inch squares. Insert a wooden pick or short bamboo skewer through the stack in the middle of each square. Beat egg and milk in a pie plate until blended. Toss breadcrumbs and cheese together; spread on waxed paper. Dip each skewered sandwich cube in egg mixture, coating all sides. Roll sandwiches in crumb mixture. Heat butter or margarine and oil in a skillet. Fry sandwiches in skillet until lightly browned on all sides. Drain on paper towels. Serve warm. Makes 20 appetizer servings.

Oregon Filbert Bisque

Filberts, also known as hazelnuts, are an Oregon treasure.

1-1/3 cups shelled filberts	1/8 teaspoon ground allspice
3 tablespoons butter or margarine	1/8 teaspoon ground nutmeg
1/4 cup all-purpose flour	1/8 teaspoon white pepper
3 cups Chicken Broth, page 16, or 1-1/2 (14-1/2-oz.) cans regular-strength chicken broth	1/2 teaspoon salt
	1/4 cup dry sherry, if desired
	1/2 cup whipped cream, if desired
2 cups milk	Freshly grated or ground nutmeg, if desired

Preheat oven to 250F (120C). Spread filberts on a 15" x 10" jelly-roll pan. Toast in oven 30 to 40 minutes, stirring occasionally. Place toasted nuts on a clean cloth towel. Rub towel and nuts together to remove as much of nut skins as possible. Finely chop nuts, 1/2 cup at a time, in a blender or all at once in a food processor. In a 3-quart saucepan, melt butter or margarine; stir in flour. Slowly add broth, stirring constantly. Add milk, stirring over medium heat until thickened and bubbles appear around pan edges. Add allspice, nutmeg, pepper, salt, chopped nuts and sherry, if desired. Simmer 5 minutes. Do not boil. Ladle hot soup into individual bowls. Top each serving with a dollop of whipped cream and a sprinkling of nutmeg, if desired. Makes 6 (3/4-cup) servings.

Do not allow soups containing milk, eggs, cream or sour cream to boil. Cook over low heat and stir frequently.

Quick Lunches

Lunchtime is short because of busy schedules with work, school and errand-running. But a nutritious meal is important for keeping you or the family going. Soups and sandwiches make the ideal quick breaks. The recipes in this chapter are ready to serve in 20 minutes or less, and they are packed with the nutritional goodness of a hot meal. A quick lunch of soup or sandwich is easy to prepare for yourself or the family to break up an active weekday at home or at the office. Weekend lunches are often crammed between activities such as baseball games and shopping. A soup or sandwich may be just what the family needs. Although they're called *lunch* soups and sandwiches, the recipes included here also make exceptional light suppers.

Lunch soups start with convenience foods to make them quick and simple. Added vegetables and seasonings give them a fresh homemade taste in no time. Canned soups are the base for Bayou Gumbo and Swiss Tomato-Mushroom Soup. Neither one tastes like anything you'll find in a can. Frozen hash-brown potatoes, canned cream-style corn and dried beef

make Navajo Corn Chowder ready to eat in 20 minutes.

Lunchtime sandwich recipes include traditional favorites—from clubs to grilled sandwiches to subs. Some are hot and some are cold, but all are best eaten freshly prepared. These sandwiches don't pack well for picnics or brown bags. The Bombay-Club Sandwich is a triple-decker for sophisticated tastes. Ham, a grilled pineapple ring, sharp Cheddar cheese and chutney are layered with toasted whole-wheat bread. A delicious combination of tuna, artichoke hearts, mushrooms and cheese fills flaky croissants for Tuna-Artichoke Horns. The sandwich is served hot with a cream-cheese sauce.

Quick sandwiches are also a welcome after-school snack, especially for always-hungry teenagers. They can prepare Pepperoni Pitas themselves by covering rounds of pita bread with their favorite pizza toppings.

Below are menus for soup and sandwich lunches your family will rush home to enjoy. When lunch includes both soup and sandwich, plan half-servings of each. ❧

Menu

Blustery-Day Lunch

Navajo Corn Chowder, page 80
Turkey Melt, page 80
Orange Wedges & Banana Slices
with Pineapple Yogurt

Mid-Day Relaxer

Swiss Tomato-Mushroom Soup, page 80
Charlie Chan Tuna Wedges, page 79
Pear Slices & Melon Balls

Tortilla Soup

A quick light soup; add a green salad and fruit to complete the meal.

4 (6-inch) corn tortillas
Oil for frying
1 (12-oz.) can tomato juice
1 (10-1/2-oz.) can concentrated beef broth
1 cup water
1 teaspoon Worcestershire sauce

3 tablespoons canned diced green chilies
1-1/4 cups creamed cottage cheese (10 oz.)
1/3 cup diced green bell pepper
2 green onions, including 2 inches of
    green tops, sliced

Cut tortillas in wedges. Pour oil to a 1-inch depth in a large skillet. Heat oil until a tortilla wedge sizzles when added and browns in 60 seconds. Do not allow oil to smoke. Fry tortilla wedges in hot oil until crisp. Drain on paper towels. In a 3-quart saucepan, combine tomato juice, broth, water, Worcestershire sauce and green chilies. Bring to a boil, stirring occasionally. Cover and simmer 10 minutes. Place 1/4 cup cottage cheese in each bowl. Sprinkle about 1 tablespoon green bell pepper and 1 teaspoon green onion over each portion of cottage cheese. Divide tortilla wedges between 5 shallow bowls. Ladle soup over tortilla wedges. Serve immediately. Makes 5 (1-cup) servings.

How to Make Tortilla Soup

1/Place tortilla wedges in each bowl.

2/Ladle soup over tortilla wedges.

Charlie Chan Tuna Wedges

A triple-decker tuna sandwich with an exotic Eastern touch.

2 (6-1/2-oz.) cans tuna, drained
2 celery stalks, sliced
1 (8-oz.) can sliced water chestnuts,
    drained
1 hard-cooked egg, chopped
1/3 cup mayonnaise

1/4 cup plain yogurt
Pinch onion salt
Pinch red (cayenne) pepper
6 slices raisin bread
1/3 cup Mango Chutney, page 34,
    or other chutney

Place tuna in a medium bowl; flake with a fork. Add celery, water chestnuts and chopped egg; toss. In a small bowl, blend mayonnaise and yogurt. Season with onion salt and red pepper. Add mayonnaise mixture to tuna mixture. Stir until ingredients are well coated with dressing. Cut bread slices in half diagonally. Spoon tuna mixture on 4 half-slices. Spread remaining 8 half-slices with chutney. Place 1 half-slice on each tuna-covered slice, chutney-side down. Spoon more tuna on top of sandwiches. Top with remaining 4 half-slices, chutney-side down. Press down on top of sandwiches. Cut each sandwich in half, corner to center of opposite side. Place 2 triangles, crust-sides down, on each of 4 individual plates. Makes 4 servings.

Mississippi Meatball Burgoo   *Photo on page 25.*

Burgoo is a Southern name for a thick, stew-like soup.

Animal Crackers, page 24, if desired
1 tablespoon butter or margarine
1 medium, green bell pepper, diced
1/2 cup chopped onion
1 garlic clove, minced
1/2 teaspoon dried leaf basil
2 tablespoons chopped fresh parsley or
    1-1/2 teaspoons dried leaf parsley

2 (10-1/2-oz.) cans Meatball Alphabet Soup
1 (10-1/2-oz.) can concentrated beef broth
1 (16-oz.) can golden hominy, drained
1 (16-oz.) can dark-red kidney beans
Dairy sour cream, if desired

Prepare Animal Crackers, if desired. Melt butter or margarine in a 3-quart saucepan. Add green pepper, onion and garlic. Sauté over medium-high heat until onion is tender. Sprinkle basil and parsley over vegetables. Add soup, broth, hominy and beans with liquid; stir to combine. Cover and simmer 10 minutes. Ladle hot soup into individual bowls. Top each serving with Animal Crackers or a dollop of sour cream, if desired. Makes 5 (1-1/2-cup) servings.

For main-dish soups, plan 1-1/2 to 2 cups per serving.

Swiss Tomato-Mushroom Soup

Ready to serve in just 15 minutes!

1 (16-oz.) can whole tomatoes
1 (10-1/2-oz.) can condensed cream-of-
   mushroom soup
1 tablespoon chopped chives or
   2 tablespoons sliced green onion

1/4 teaspoon sugar
1/8 teaspoon pepper
1/2 cup dairy sour cream
1 cup shredded Swiss cheese (4 oz.)

Puree tomatoes with liquid in a blender or food processor. Combine pureed tomatoes, condensed soup, chives or green onion, sugar and pepper in a medium saucepan. Heat until mixture begins to boil. Stir in sour cream. Stir over low heat until heated through, 2 to 3 minutes. Do not boil. Stir in cheese. Ladle hot soup into individual bowls. Makes 4 (1-cup) servings.

Navajo Corn Chowder

Dried beef is very salty; no additional salt needs to be added to the chowder.

1 tablespoon butter or margarine
1/2 cup chopped onion
1 tablespoon all-purpose flour
2-1/2 cups milk
1 (17-oz.) can cream-style corn

1 (2-1/2-oz.) jar dried beef, cut in strips
3 tablespoons vegetable oil
2 cups frozen Southern-style
   hash-brown potatoes
Corn chips or CornNuts

Melt butter or margarine in a 3-quart saucepan. Add onion; sauté over medium-high heat until tender. Stir in flour until blended. Gradually add milk, stirring constantly. Add corn and dried beef. Simmer 10 minutes, stirring occasionally. Do not boil. Heat oil in a large skillet. Add potatoes. Cook over medium-low heat, turning potatoes occasionally, until tender, about 10 minutes. Add potatoes to saucepan. Serve steaming hot chowder with corn chips or CornNuts floating on top. Makes 4 (1-1/2-cup) servings.

Turkey Melt

A day-after-Thanksgiving or year-round delight with home-cooked or deli-sliced turkey.

8 slices Herb Bread, page 56,
   Home-Style White Bread, page 33, or
   other firm-textured bread
1/3 cup Savory Butter, page 36,
   butter or margarine, room temperature

4 oz. Edam or Gouda cheese, sliced
8 oz. sliced cooked turkey
1/2 cup cranberry-orange relish

Spread both sides of 4 slices of bread with Savory Butter, butter or margarine. Arrange cheese and turkey on each slice. Spread about 2 tablespoons relish over turkey. Spread remaining 4 slices bread on 1 side with Savory Butter, butter or margarine. Place on top of sandwiches, buttered-side up. Grill sandwiches on a griddle or in a large skillet until golden brown on both sides. Serve warm. Makes 4 servings.

Sandwich Loaf Italiano *Photo on cover.*

An unusual sandwich with a distinctive Italian flavor.

1 loaf Cheddar-Cheese Bread, page 38, Herb Bread, page 56, or Italian bread	1/4 teaspoon dried Italian herb seasoning
1/3 cup butter or margarine, room temperature	1/4 cup freshly grated Parmesan cheese (3/4 oz.)
1 garlic clove, minced	1 large green bell pepper
1/2 teaspoon seasoned salt	8 slices salami (about 8 oz.)
	8 slices provolone cheese (about 8 oz.)

Preheat oven to 350F (175C). Cut bread almost through into 16 slices, leaving bottom of loaf uncut. In a small bowl, combine butter or margarine, garlic, seasoned salt, Italian seasoning and Parmesan cheese. Cream with the back of a spoon until well mixed. Spread butter or margarine mixture on cut surfaces facing each other on the first 2 bread slices. Do not butter next 2 surfaces. Butter next 2 surfaces facing each other. Repeat to end of loaf. Cut green pepper crosswise in 8 thin slices. Remove and discard seeds. Arrange 1 slice salami, 1 slice provolone cheese and 1 slice green pepper between each buttered slice. Wrap loaf loosely in foil. Bake 15 minutes. Serve in a basket or on a bread board. Separate loaf into 8 sandwiches. Makes 8 servings.

Tuna-Artichoke Horns

A warm sandwich in a flaky croissant that's ready to eat in 15 minutes.

1 (6-1/2-oz.) can tuna, drained	1/2 cup dairy sour cream
1 (6-oz.) jar marinated artichoke hearts, drained, chopped	3 tablespoons milk
1 (3-oz.) can whole mushrooms, drained	1 bunch fresh spinach or romaine lettuce
1 cup shredded Swiss cheese (4 oz.)	1 tablespoon snipped fresh chives or sliced green onion
4 Croissants, page 44, or other croissants	2 radishes, thinly sliced
1 (3-oz.) pkg. cream cheese with chives	

Preheat oven to 350F (175C). In a small bowl, combine tuna, artichoke hearts, mushrooms and Swiss cheese; toss together. Split croissants horizontally. Open and place on a baking sheet. Fill croissants with tuna mixture. Replace tops. Bake 10 minutes. In a small saucepan, heat together cream cheese, sour cream and milk. Stir constantly until smooth and bubbly. Remove from heat. Cover luncheon plates with spinach or romaine lettuce. Place 1 croissant on each plate. Remove top and set at an angle at back of bottom part. Spoon warm cream sauce over filling. Sprinkle with chives or green onion. Arrange several radish slices beside sandwiches. Serve immediately. Makes 4 servings.

Salad-Bar Sub

All your favorite salad-bar fixin's piled on French bread.

4 hard-cooked eggs, chopped
2 green onions, sliced
1/8 teaspoon salt
Pinch white pepper
1/4 cup mayonnaise
1 (1-lb.) loaf French bread,
   about 16 inches long
Spicy Tomato Mustard, page 48,
   or other mustard

3 large lettuce leaves
1 small cucumber, peeled, thinly sliced
3 small tomatoes, thinly sliced
1 avocado
1 cup alfalfa sprouts
1/2 cup ranch-style salad dressing
1/3 cup roasted hulled sunflower seeds
Dill-pickle slices, if desired
Pimiento-stuffed olives, if desired

In a medium bowl, combine eggs, green onions, salt, white pepper and mayonnaise. Split French bread lengthwise. Separate parts. Spread each with mustard. Arrange lettuce leaves on bottom part of loaf. Spoon egg mixture onto lettuce leaves; spread to cover. Arrange alternating cucumber and tomato slices, overlapping slightly, on egg salad. Cut avocado in lengthwise slices. Arrange slices, diagonally, across vegetables. Separate sprouts; scatter over sandwich. Drizzle salad dressing over the top. Sprinkle sunflower seeds over sprouts. Place top slice of loaf, mustard-side down, on sandwich. Press on the top. Cut loaf in 4-inch segments. Place a wooden pick with several pickle slices and 1 olive in the top of each serving, if desired. Makes 4 servings.

Bayou Gumbo

Canned chicken-gumbo soup contains okra, the essential ingredient in gumbo, a Creole specialty.

1 tablespoon butter or margarine
1 small green bell pepper, diced
1/2 cup chopped onion
1 (10-1/2-oz.) can condensed
   Manhattan-style clam chowder
1 (10-1/2-oz.) can condensed
   chicken-gumbo soup

2 cups water
1/4 teaspoon dried leaf thyme
1/4 cup uncooked long-grain rice
1 cup cooked, frozen or canned small shrimp

Melt butter or margarine in a 3-quart saucepan. Add green pepper and onion. Sauté over medium-high heat until onion is tender. Add condensed chowder and soup, water and thyme. Bring to a boil. Sprinkle rice into boiling soup mixture. Reduce heat to low. Cover and simmer 15 minutes. Add shrimp; simmer 5 minutes longer. Ladle hot soup into individual bowls. Makes 4 (1-1/2-cup) servings.

Salad-Bar Sub

South Seas Fruit Pockets

Tropical papaya, kiwi and banana make a cooling summer lunch.

1/3 cup Honey-Lemon Dressing, see below	2 bananas
1 avocado	4 whole-wheat pita-bread rounds
1 tablespoon lemon juice	2 cups alfalfa sprouts
1 papaya	1/4 cup hulled sunflower seeds
2 kiwi	

Honey-Lemon Dressing:

3 tablespoons honey	1/4 teaspoon salt
2 tablespoons lemon juice	1/4 teaspoon dry mustard
1/2 teaspoon grated onion	1/4 cup vegetable oil

Prepare Honey-Lemon Dressing. Cut avocado in 1/2-inch cubes. Toss avocado cubes in lemon juice until coated on all sides. Cut papaya in half. Scoop out seeds with a spoon; discard seeds. Peel papaya halves. Cut each half, crosswise, in 1/4-inch slices. Cut long slices of papaya in half to make 2'' x 1/4'' pieces. Peel kiwi. Cut crosswise in thin rounds. Slice bananas. Combine avocado, papaya, kiwi and bananas in a medium bowl. Pour 1/3 cup Honey-Lemon Dressing over fruit; toss to coat fruit. Cover and refrigerate until ready to serve, up to 2 hours. Cut bread rounds in half. To serve, stir sprouts and sunflower seeds into fruit mixture. Stuff fruit into pocket rounds. Arrange 2 stuffed pockets on each plate. Makes 4 servings.

Honey-Lemon Dressing:
Combine all ingredients in a 1-pint jar with a tight-fitting lid. Shake vigorously about 30 seconds. Makes about 1/2 cup.

Variation
Honey-Lime Dressing: Substitute lime juice for lemon juice.

Pepperoni Pitas

Kids can make these as an after-school snack.

1 (8-oz.) can pizza sauce	1/4 cup canned sliced mushrooms, drained
4 pita-bread rounds	2 oz. pepperoni, sliced
1 cup shredded mozzarella cheese (4 oz.)	12 pitted ripe olives, sliced

Simmer pizza sauce in a small saucepan 5 minutes. Preheat oven to 400F (205C). Flatten bread rounds if necessary by cutting a small slit along 1 edge and pressing on the top to remove air pockets. Place bread rounds on a baking sheet. For each pita, spread about 1/4 cup pizza sauce over surface. Sprinkle about 1 tablespoon cheese over sauce. Arrange mushroom slices, pepperoni and olives on bread rounds. Sprinkle with remaining cheese. Bake until cheese melts and sauce is bubbling, about 15 minutes. Makes 4 servings.

How to Make Bombay-Club Sandwiches

1/Place pineapple on baking sheet or toaster-oven tray. Sprinkle with brown sugar. Broil until hot and bubbling.

2/Arrange ham slices on 4 spread-covered bread slices. Top with pineapple rings and complete sandwiches.

Bombay-Club Sandwiches

An American invention, the club is a three-layer sandwich.

1/3 cup Tangy-Sweet Spread, page 46
4 pineapple rings, fresh or canned
1 tablespoon brown sugar
12 slices Sesame-Whole-Wheat Bread,
    page 55, or other whole-wheat bread

8 oz. sliced ham
4 oz. sharp Cheddar cheese, sliced
1/2 cup Mango Chutney, page 34,
    or other chutney

Prepare Tangy-Sweet Spread. Preheat broiler or toaster oven. Place pineapple rings on a baking sheet or toaster-oven tray. Sprinkle pineapple lightly with brown sugar. Broil pineapple until hot and bubbling. Toast bread. Spread 8 slices generously with Tangy-Sweet Spread. Arrange ham slices on 4 spread-covered bread slices. Top ham with pineapple rings. Place remaining slices of spread-covered toast on pineapple rings, spread-side down. Arrange cheese slices on top of sandwiches. Spread remaining toast slices with chutney. Place on top of sandwiches, chutney-side down. Cut sandwiches diagonally, corner to corner, in both directions. Arrange triangles on individual plates. Makes 4 servings.

Picnics & Packed Lunches

hen warm sunny days come, parks and back-yards are filled with the shouts and cheers of outdoor games. Picnic tables are loaded with a variety of favorite foods. A picnic can be as big as a family reunion with food for 50 or as simple as a week-end lunch for one. Though picnics come to mind with spring and summer weather, a bone-warming break on the ski-trail should not be forgotten. Take a thermos of Lentil with Lemon Soup or hot Corned-Beef Picnic Buns wrapped in foil for a picnic in the snow.

Picnics provide a chance to get out of our daily work-ing surroundings to relax and enjoy ourselves. The per-fect setting might be a tree-lined grassy hill, a rocky secluded beach or a blanket in the family room in front of a roaring fire. Brown-bag lunchers can create the set-ting in their minds to escape the hectic pace of the morning.

Soups and sandwiches fit any picnic occasion. Wel-come a family to the neighborhood with a backyard barbecue featuring Corn Dogs and Tomato-Seafood Bisque. Carry Picnic Tacos to a local orchard to enjoy apple-blossom time. Or, plan a Christmas picnic around the tree with Navy-Bean Soup.

Soups and sandwiches provide easy fare for picnics and packed lunches. They can be served hot for an outing on a cold, blustery day, or chilled and crisp to cool the hottest dog day. An efficient thermos will keep soups at hot or cold serving temperature up to three hours.

You can help your thermos do a good job of keeping hot soups and sandwich fillings hot. While the soup or sandwich filling heats, prewarm the thermos by filling it with boiling water. Let it stand for three to five min-utes then pour out the water and fill with the hot soup

or filling. Try to time it so the thermos is filled as close as possible to your departure. Wrap hot turnovers and buns tightly in foil and provide plenty of insulation. Newspaper or a towel wrapped around the foil will help keep the heat in. For additional insulation, styrofoam chests can be used as warmers as well as coolers.

Soups to be served cold can be carried in a thermos or packed in ice in an ice chest. Be sure the soup is well chilled before packing. Allow at least eight hours in the refrigerator. Chilling the thermos for an hour or two will keep the soup cold longer.

Sandwiches can be prepared in advance for the easi-est picnic or put together as needed. Bread, spreads, fillings and a knife take up little more space than the finished sandwiches.

Sandwiches prepared ahead can be carried in plastic containers with lids or wrapped in foil or plastic wrap. Frozen sandwiches work well for packed lunches. Refer to page 9 for how to freeze sandwiches. Pack sandwiches straight from the freezer into lunch boxes or a picnic basket. By lunchtime, they will be ready to eat.

Most sandwiches will stay soft and flavorful for several hours in almost any weather. But sandwiches containing fillings made with mayonnaise, eggs or cream cheese must be kept in an ice chest or cooler. Do not add lettuce, tomato, sprouts or special dress-ings to sandwiches to be packed. Place these crisp or juicy extras in their own containers to be added im-mediately before the sandwiches are eaten.

Even well-packed soups and sandwiches won't stay hot long enough to warm chilled hands or stay cool, crisp and flavorful for long. Plan to enjoy your specially prepared picnic fare within four hours. ❧

Red-Wine Gazpacho
Photo on pages 88 and 89.

Adds something special to a picnic at the beach or on the back patio.

Chili-Pepper Croutons, page 24, if desired
4 large tomatoes
2 (12-oz.) cans tomato juice
2 tablespoons olive oil
3/4 cup dry red wine
1 tablespoon red-wine vinegar
1/2 teaspoon salt
1 teaspoon paprika
Pinch sugar

2 tablespoons chopped cilantro or
   1/2 teaspoon dried leaf oregano
1/4 cup canned diced green chilies
2 to 4 drops hot-pepper sauce
2 green onions, sliced
1/2 medium cucumber, peeled, shredded
1/3 cup diced green bell pepper
1 (2-oz.) can sliced black olives, drained
1 (3-3/4-oz.) can whole oysters, if desired

Prepare Chili-Pepper Croutons, if desired. Bring a small amount of water to a boil. Place tomatoes in boiling water for 30 seconds. Remove from boiling water and cover with cold water. Peel and core tomatoes; cut in half crosswise. Remove and discard seeds; dice tomatoes. In a large bowl or plastic container, stir together diced tomatoes, tomato juice, olive oil, wine, vinegar, salt, paprika, sugar, cilantro or oregano and green chilies. Add hot-pepper sauce to taste. Stir in green onions, cucumber, green pepper, black olives and oysters, if desired. Cover and refrigerate at least 4 hours. Serve chilled gazpacho with Chili-Pepper Croutons sprinkled on top, if desired. Makes 4 (1-1/2-cup) servings.

Potato-Salad Soup
Photo on pages 88 and 89.

For a picnic, keep well-chilled on ice until ready to serve.

4 medium potatoes, peeled, diced
3 cups water
1 teaspoon salt
1/3 cup chopped onion
3 tablespoons butter or margarine
1/4 cup sliced green onions
1 cup sliced celery
3 tablespoons all-purpose flour

2-1/2 cups milk
1 egg
1 cup half and half
1/4 cup white-wine vinegar
1/2 cup mayonnaise
1/3 cup pickle relish
2 hard-cooked eggs

Combine potatoes, water, salt and onion in a large saucepan. Bring to a boil; reduce heat to low. Cover and simmer until potatoes are tender, about 20 minutes. Melt butter or margarine in a 4-quart pot. Add green onions and celery. Sauté over medium heat until green onions are tender. Sprinkle flour over sautéed vegetables; stir to combine. Slowly pour in milk, stirring constantly. Bring to a boil, stirring constantly until thickened. Stir in potatoes and their cooking liquid. In a small bowl, combine egg and half and half; slowly pour egg mixture into thickened soup, stirring constantly. Reduce heat to low. Cook 5 minutes, stirring occasionally. Do not boil. Remove from heat. Stir in vinegar, mayonnaise and pickle relish. Separate white and yolk of hard-cooked eggs. Dice egg whites; stir into soup mixture. Press egg yolks through a sieve; set aside for garnish. Pour soup into a large bowl or container with a lid. Cover and refrigerate soup and egg yolks at least 4 hours. To serve, ladle cold soup into individual bowls or mugs. Sprinkle sieved egg yolk over each serving. Makes 6 (1-1/2-cup) servings.

Shown on the following pages from left to right: Potato-Salad Soup; Red-Wine Gazpacho; Picnic Sticks, page 90; and Deli Rolls, page 95.

Picnic Sticks   Photo on pages 88 and 89.

Fun to eat because the bread is on the inside!

4 slices bologna, summer sausage, salami or
   other cold-cut
1/3 cup processed cheese spread with bacon,
   room temperature
12 (3-inch) breadsticks
4 square slices sandwich ham
4 thin slices Jarlsberg or Swiss cheese

2 tablespoons Spicy Tomato Mustard,
   page 48, or other mustard
4 thin slices roast beef
1/3 cup Pepper-Cheese Spread, page 47, or
   processed cheese spread with jalapeño
   peppers, room temperature

Lay bologna or cold-cut slices on a flat surface. Spoon a generous 1 tablespoon cheese spread over each slice. Place a breadstick on edge of each slice; roll up. Lay ham slices on a flat surface. Arrange cheese slices on ham. Spread cheese with a thin layer of mustard. Place a breadstick at 1 edge of each ham slice; roll up. Lay roast beef slices on a flat surface. Spoon a generous 1 tablespoon Pepper-Cheese Spread or other cheese spread over each beef slice. Place a breadstick at 1 edge of each slice; roll up. Wrap Picnic Sticks in plastic wrap or foil, or enclose in a plastic container. Carry to picnic in an ice chest. Makes 12 sticks or 4 servings.

Tomato-Seafood Bisque

Shrimp, clams, oysters or a combination of seafood make this bisque elegant picnic fare.

Cracker Balls, page 23, or oyster crackers
2 tablespoons butter or margarine
1/2 medium onion, sliced
1/2 medium, green bell pepper, diced
1 carrot, shredded
1/4 cup all-purpose flour
1 teaspoon salt

1/2 teaspoon paprika
1/8 teaspoon pepper
1 (16-oz.) can whole tomatoes
1 cup cooked small shrimp, clams, oysters or
   a combination of seafood
2 cups milk
2 tablespoons dry sherry

Prepare Cracker Balls, if using. Melt butter or margarine in a 4-quart pot. Add onion, green pepper and carrot. Sauté over medium-high heat until onion is tender. Remove from heat. Sprinkle flour, salt, paprika and pepper over sautéed vegetables; stir until coated. Press tomatoes and liquid through a sieve. Gradually pour sieved tomatoes into vegetable mixture, stirring constantly. Return pot to heat. Bring mixture to a boil, stirring constantly. Add shrimp, clams, oysters or combination of seafood. Cover and simmer 5 minutes. Heat milk in a small saucepan until bubbles form around edges of pan. Pour milk into hot soup, stirring constantly. Stir in sherry. Ladle hot soup into a warmed thermos. Serve hot in mugs. Top individual servings with Cracker Balls or oyster crackers. Makes 5 (1-cup) servings.

How to Make Corned-Beef Picnic Buns

1/Pull up sides of dough over filling. Roll to opposite point of triangle until filling is completely covered.

2/Serve buns warm or at room temperature.

Corned-Beef Picnic Buns

Extra buns can be stored in the refrigerator and reheated for tomorrow's lunch.

6 oz. cooked corned beef, chopped
2 tablespoons chili sauce
1/4 cup mayonnaise
1 tablespoon pickle relish
1 tablespoon finely chopped onion

2 oz. Monterey Jack cheese, diced
1 (8-oz.) can refrigerated crescent rolls
1-1/2 teaspoons butter or margarine, melted
1/2 cup crushed potato chips

Preheat oven to 375F (190C). Grease 8 muffin cups. In a bowl, combine corned beef, chili sauce, mayonnaise, pickle relish, onion and cheese. Separate refrigerated dough into triangles. Place about 2 tablespoons corned-beef mixture on each dough triangle near wide end. Pull up sides of dough over filling. Roll to opposite point of triangle until filling is completely covered. Pinch edges to seal. Place buns in greased muffin cups with point of dough on the bottom. Brush tops with butter or margarine. Sprinkle potato chips over buns. Gently press chips into buns. Bake until lightly browned, about 20 minutes. Cool slightly on a rack. Wrap warm buns in paper napkins or paper towels. Serve warm or at room temperature. If buns will not be served within 3 hours, refrigerate. Reheat buns on a baking sheet in a 350F (175C) oven 10 minutes. Makes 8 servings.

Corn Dogs

Reheat on a grill at the picnic site or serve while still warm.

1 cup all-purpose flour
1 cup cornmeal
1 tablespoon baking powder
1 teaspoon salt
1/4 cup shortening
1 egg
2/3 cup milk

1/2 cup cornmeal
6 hot dogs
Oil for deep-frying
Ketchup
Spicy Tomato Mustard, page 48, or
   other mustard

Combine flour, 1 cup cornmeal, baking powder and salt in a bowl. Using a pastry blender, cut in shortening until mixture resembles coarse meal. In a small bowl, beat egg and milk. Pour egg mixture into dry ingredients. Stir until barely mixed. Sprinkle 1/2 cup cornmeal on a sheet of waxed paper. Insert a wooden skewer in each hot dog. Place hot dogs, 1 at a time, in cornmeal dough. Using a spoon, form dough around hot dogs. Roll hot dogs in cornmeal. Continue shaping with your hands until hot dogs are completely covered and smooth. Pour oil to a 1-inch depth in a large skillet. Heat oil to 350F (175C) or until a 1-inch cube of bread added to oil turns brown in 60 seconds. Carefully put hot dogs in hot oil. Fry until golden brown, turning frequently, 3 to 5 minutes. Drain on paper towels; cool. Wrap cooled Corn Dogs in paper napkins or paper towels. Do not wrap tightly in plastic wrap or foil or Corn Dogs will soften. Serve with ketchup and mustard. Makes 6 servings.

Tuna-Cheese Puffs

Cheese puffs may be prepared ahead and stored without filling for two to three days.

1 cup water
1/3 cup butter or margarine
1 cup sifted bread flour or
   all-purpose flour
1/2 cup shredded Cheddar cheese (2 oz.)
4 eggs
1 (6-1/2-oz.) can tuna, drained

1 (6-oz.) jar marinated artichoke hearts
2 tablespoons sliced black olives
1 celery stalk, sliced
2 green onions, sliced
1 teaspoon wine vinegar
1 tablespoon Champagne Mustard,
   page 40, or Dijon-style mustard

Preheat oven to 400F (205C). Bring water to a boil in a medium saucepan. Add butter or margarine. When butter or margarine has melted, add flour all at once. Stir over medium heat until dough forms a ball. Stir in cheese. Remove from heat. Add eggs, 1 at a time, beating after each addition, until dough is smooth. Spoon about 1/3 cup dough onto a baking sheet; form into a ball. Repeat with remaining dough, making 6 balls. Bake until balls puff and are golden brown, about 30 minutes. Remove from oven. Cut a slice off top of each puff. Cool. Store puffs, loosely covered, at room temperature. Place tuna in a small bowl. Flake tuna with a fork. Drain artichoke hearts, reserving marinade. Cut hearts in quarters. Add quartered artichokes, olives, celery and green onions to tuna. Add vinegar and mustard to reserved marinade. Pour marinade over tuna mixture. Toss to coat ingredients well. Spoon tuna filling into cooled cheese puffs. Replace tops. Wrap in paper napkins or towels. Serve within 3 hours. Makes 6 servings.

How to Make Corn Dogs

1/Insert a wooden skewer in each hot dog. Using a spoon, form dough around hot dogs.

2/Roll hot dogs in cornmeal. Shape with your hands until completely covered and smooth.

Pacific-Salmon Rolls

Salmon patties, wrapped in foil, will stay warm two to three hours.

1 (15-oz.) can salmon
1 cup dry breadcrumbs or cracker crumbs
1/2 teaspoon dried dillweed
1/4 cup shredded Swiss cheese (1 oz.)
1 egg
1/4 cup mayonnaise
2 drops hot-pepper sauce

1 teaspoon Champagne Mustard, page 40,
  or Dijon-style mustard
1 tablespoon butter or margarine
1 tablespoon vegetable oil
4 Seeded Kaiser Rolls, page 48, Hamburger
  Buns, page 33, or other sandwich rolls
1/4 cup Special Hamburger Sauce, page 33

Drain salmon, discarding liquid. Remove and discard bones. Flake salmon with a fork. In a medium bowl, combine salmon, crumbs, dillweed and cheese; toss to mix. In another bowl, beat together egg, mayonnaise, hot-pepper sauce and mustard. Combine egg mixture and salmon mixture. Shape into 4 patties, about 1/2 inch thick. Heat butter or margarine and oil in a large skillet over medium heat until butter or margarine melts. Add salmon patties. Fry until lightly browned, about 3 minutes on each side. Slightly cool patties. Wrap in foil. To serve, spread split rolls or buns generously with Special Hamburger Sauce. Place 1 patty in each bun. Makes 4 servings.

Picnic Tacos

Pack hot chili and mixed taco salad separately to make the tacos when it's time for lunch.

8 Taco Shells, see below, or
    other taco shells
1/2 lb. ground beef
1 small garlic clove, minced
1/4 teaspoon salt
2 tablespoons all-purpose flour
1 tablespoon chili powder
1/4 teaspoon ground cumin
1 cup Beef Broth, page 14, or
    canned regular-strength beef broth

1 cup drained, cooked pinto beans or
    1/2 (15-oz.) can pinto beans, drained
2 cups shredded lettuce
1 medium tomato, diced
8 pitted black olives, sliced
1 cup shredded Cheddar cheese (4 oz.)
Bottled taco sauce, if desired

Taco Shells:
Oil for frying
8 (6-inch) corn tortillas

Prepare Taco Shells. Brown ground beef in a medium skillet until no longer pink. Drain off pan drippings. Add garlic and salt to beef. In a small bowl, combine flour, chili powder and cumin; sprinkle over meat. Stir to combine. Slowly add broth, stirring constantly. Bring to a boil, stirring constantly. Add beans; simmer until heated through, about 10 minutes. Ladle hot mixture into a warmed thermos. In a medium bowl, combine lettuce, tomato, olives and cheese. Sprinkle taco sauce over lettuce mixture if desired; toss lightly. Place lettuce mixture in an airtight container or plastic bag. Place cooled taco shells in a plastic container to prevent breakage. To serve, spoon hot chili into a taco shell. Spread lettuce mixture over chili. Makes 8 servings.

Taco Shells:
Heat 1-1/2 inches oil in a deep heavy skillet over medium-high heat until a piece of tortilla sizzles when added and browns in 60 seconds. Using a taco-fryer or tongs, fry tortillas in a folded taco shape until crisp. If using a taco fryer, place tortilla in opened fryer so middle of tortilla is at bottom of curve. Close fryer, sandwiching tortilla. Lay fryer flat on its side in hot oil. Fry until crisp and golden. Turn and fry other side. Drain on paper towels. If using tongs, place 1 tortilla in hot oil to soften; turn over. Lift 1 edge of tortilla with tongs. Fold in half, still holding edge out of oil. Fry until crisp and golden. Turn taco shell. Fry, holding crisp edge out of oil. Place a cooling rack over paper towels. Invert taco shells over rack to prevent shells from closing; drain. Repeat using remaining tortillas. Set aside until ready to use.

How to Make Picnic Tacos

1/Place a tortilla in hot oil to soften; using tongs, turn tortilla.

2/Lift edge of tortilla with tongs. Fold in half, holding edge out of oil.

Deli Rolls   Photo on pages 88 and 89.

Prepare at breakfast; by lunchtime the zesty dressing will have flavored the roll.

1 (8-oz.) can garbanzo beans, drained
2 oz. Swiss cheese, cut in julienne strips
2 oz. Cheddar cheese, cut in julienne strips
2 oz. ham, cut in julienne strips
2 oz. roast beef, cut in julienne strips

1/4 cup pimiento-stuffed sliced olives
1/3 cup bottled Italian salad dressing
1 tablespoon Champagne Mustard,
    page 40, or Dijon-style mustard
4 round crisp rolls

In a medium bowl, combine garbanzo beans, cheeses, ham, roast beef and olives; toss to mix. In a small bowl, combine salad dressing and mustard; pour over bean mixture. Toss until ingredients are coated. Refrigerate until ready to use. Cut a slice off the top of each hard roll. Hollow out roll, leaving a 1/2-inch shell. Spoon bean mixture into rolls; replace tops. Wrap in plastic wrap or foil. Leave rolls at room temperature at least 30 minutes before serving. Makes 4 servings.

Lentil with Lemon Soup

A hearty, warming soup for picnics in the snow.

1-1/2 cups dried lentils
2 bacon slices
1 cup chopped onion
2 medium carrots, sliced
1 celery stalk, sliced
1 garlic clove, minced
6 cups water
1 teaspoon grated lemon peel

1 bay leaf
1-1/2 teaspoons salt
1 large potato, peeled, diced
3 tablespoons lemon juice
1 teaspoon ground cumin
4 large Swiss-chard leaves or
    fresh spinach leaves, shredded

Sort and rinse lentils; place in a 4-quart pot. Fry bacon in a large skillet until crisp; drain and cool on paper towels. Reserve 2 tablespoons bacon drippings, discarding remainder. Crumble cooked bacon. Add onion, carrots, celery and garlic to reserved drippings in skillet. Sauté over medium-high heat until onion is tender. Add sautéed vegetables to lentils. Stir in water, lemon peel, bay leaf, salt and diced potato. Bring to a boil; reduce heat. Cover and simmer until lentils are tender, about 45 minutes. Stir in crumbled bacon, lemon juice, cumin and Swiss chard or spinach. Ladle hot soup into a warmed thermos. Serve hot in mugs. Makes 5 (2-cup) servings.

Navy-Bean Soup

A favorite at home; it can be a satisfying lunch at the office.

1 lb. dried navy beans or small white beans
1 medium onion, chopped
2 garlic cloves, minced
1 small smoked ham hock
2 qts. water
1 teaspoon salt
1/4 teaspoon pepper

3/4 cup instant-potato flakes
1 cup chopped celery
2 tablespoons chopped fresh parsley or
    1/2 tablespoon dried leaf parsley
12 cocktail smoky-sausage links or
    3 regular-size sausage links,
    cut in bite-size pieces, if desired

Sort and rinse beans; place in a 4-quart pot. Cover with water to about 3 inches above beans. Soak 8 hours or overnight. Or, quick-soak by bringing beans and water to a boil. Boil 2 minutes; remove from heat. Cover and let stand 1 hour. Drain soaked beans; discarding water. Return beans to pot; stir in onion, garlic, ham hock, 2 quarts water, salt and pepper. Bring to a boil; reduce heat. Cover and simmer until beans are tender, about 1-1/2 hours. Remove ham hock; pull meat from bone. Dice meat; discard bone. Add diced meat to cooked beans. Ladle about 2 cups liquid from pot into a bowl; stir in potato flakes until smooth. Stir potato mixture into beans. Add celery and parsley. Simmer 30 minutes longer. Refrigerate soup in an airtight container until needed, up to 3 days. When reheating soup, add sausages, if desired. Ladle hot soup into a warmed thermos. Serve hot in mugs or bowls. Makes 6 (2-cup) servings.

Eating Light

Today, many of us are eating lighter meals. Heavy meat-and-potato meals do not fit with active work schedules and exercise programs which are becoming part of our lives. The soups and sandwiches that follow naturally fit into this pattern of eating. They have a light, refreshing taste and are not too filling.

Garden-Picked Pockets are stuffed with crisp, fresh vegetables in a light vinaigrette dressing. Vegetables make the sandwich satisfying and filling without adding excessive calories. Island-Paradise Soup is a cool, refreshing soup of melon, cucumber and ham in a yogurt-buttermilk base. Low-calorie, yet flavorful melon and cucumber make it ideal for a dieter's lunch.

Meats, cheeses and salad dressings are important ingredients in soups and sandwiches. Used in small amounts, they add richness and flavor without being too heavy. Low-calorie cheeses, such as mozzarella, ricotta and Neufchâtel, make sandwiches light without sacrificing flavor. Cheese & Popcorn Soup has only two ounces of extra-sharp Cheddar cheese. It is added just before serving for a rich, Cheddary taste. Lower-calorie Neufchâtel cheese gives the soup the body and creaminess a cheese soup needs. One-half slice of sandwich ham does not look skimpy on Ham & Melon Triangles. A smooth, lemony cheese spread and slices of melon so perfectly complement the ham that more is unnecessary.

Mayonnaise-type salad dressings are traditional sandwich spreads. It's just not a sandwich without a dressing—at least not a juicy, tasty sandwich. Dressings used in these recipes are made with vinegar and oil, or mayonnaise combined with yogurt, milk or buttermilk. There are also some special fruit dressings. All are lighter and lower in calories than mayonnaise alone. Yogurt and cranberry sauce as a dressing adds a tangy sweetness that's light-tasting in Turkey-Orange Open-Face.

Many of the sandwiches are open-face, using only one slice of bread. Others use no bread at all! Shrimp & Egg Ranchero Stacks pile shrimp, egg and lettuce between slices of jícama, a crunchy Mexican vegetable. Tuna-Rice Towers use puffed-rice cakes as a base. Tuna-Cheese Leaves have the sandwich filling spread between cabbage or lettuce leaves.

The soups are made with broth or skim milk, but they are not tasteless or thin. Sherried Mushroom Soup has a full mushroom flavor enhanced with a touch of sherry. Garden-Vegetable Chowder is thickened with instant potato flakes for added nutrition.

When eating smaller servings and low-calorie foods, how the meal is served becomes very important. The plate you sit down to must be colorful and attractively arranged. Low-calorie garnishes like lettuce, tomato slices or small pieces of other vegetables and fruits can fill the plate and accent the soup or sandwich. Plan to use small plates and bowls so the sandwich or soup is not lost and does not look skimpy.

Asparagus & Egg-Drop Soup

Beaten egg forms threads as it is dropped into hot soup.

1/2 lb. fresh asparagus or
   1 (9-oz.) pkg. frozen cut asparagus,
   thawed
4 green onions
1 tablespoon butter or margarine
1 tablespoon olive oil
1 garlic clove, minced
1/2 teaspoon dried leaf basil
1/4 teaspoon dried leaf thyme

1/4 teaspoon white pepper
6 cups Chicken Broth, page 16, or
   3 (14-1/2-oz.) cans regular-strength
   chicken broth
6 large romaine or escarole leaves,
   shredded
2 tablespoons chopped fresh parsley
2 eggs
2 tablespoons freshly grated Parmesan cheese

Wash fresh asparagus. Snap off heavy woody ends; discard. Cut asparagus stalks in 1-inch pieces. If using frozen asparagus, separate pieces; drain. Cut green onions in 2-inch pieces. Cut pieces lengthwise in julienne strips. Heat butter or margarine and oil in a 4-quart pot. Stir in asparagus, green-onion strips and garlic. Sauté over medium heat 2 minutes. Sprinkle basil, thyme and white pepper over sautéed vegetables. Stir in broth. Bring mixture to a boil; reduce heat to low. Cover and simmer until asparagus is tender, about 10 to 15 minutes. Add romaine or escarole and parsley. Simmer 5 minutes longer. In a medium bowl, beat eggs until well combined. Remove soup from heat. Slowly pour eggs into soup, stirring gently. Eggs will form firm threads in soup. Ladle hot soup into individual bowls. Sprinkle 1 teaspoon Parmesan cheese over each serving. Makes 6 (1-1/2-cup) servings.

Variation

Chinese Egg-Drop Soup: Substitute 6 ounces fresh edible pea pods or Chinese pea pods or 1 (6-ounce) package frozen pea pods for asparagus. Prepare soup as above.

Island-Paradise Soup

A chilled soup for hot summer days or a refreshing packed lunch.

1/2 medium cantaloupe
1/2 medium honeydew melon
1 small cucumber, peeled
2 (8-oz.) cartons plain yogurt (2 cups)
2 cups buttermilk
2 teaspoons dry ranch-style
   salad-dressing mix

1/2 teaspoon salt
Pinch white pepper
2 oz. ham, cut in cubes
2 tablespoons chopped chives or
   green onion

Using a spoon, scoop seeds from melons; discard seeds. Cut cantaloupe and honeydew in balls with a melon-baller. Thinly slice cucumber. Make cucumber rings by cutting out center seeds with a knife. Discard seeds. In a 2-quart container or casserole with a lid, stir yogurt until smooth. Gradually stir buttermilk into yogurt. Stir in dressing mix, salt and white pepper. Stir in melon balls, cucumber rings and ham cubes. Cover and refrigerate until chilled, at least 4 hours. Serve in chilled bowls. Sprinkle chopped chives or green onion over each serving. Makes 5 (1-1/2-cup) servings.

How to Make Asparagus & Egg-Drop Soup

1/Slowly pour eggs into soup, stirring gently. Eggs will form firm threads in soup.

2/Ladle hot soup into individual bowls. Sprinkle each serving with Parmesan cheese.

Turkey-Orange Open-Face

A classic team—turkey, cranberries and oranges—combine in a healthy sandwich.

2 oranges
1/2 cup plain yogurt
1/4 cup whole-cranberry sauce
4 slices Sesame-Whole-Wheat Bread,
  page 55, or other whole-wheat bread

4 red-leaf lettuce leaves
4 oz. sliced cooked turkey
1 tablespoon whole-cranberry sauce

Grate 1-1/2 teaspoons orange peel; set aside. Peel oranges, removing all white pith. Slice oranges crosswise. In a small bowl, combine yogurt, 1/4 cup whole-cranberry sauce and 1/2 teaspoon orange peel. Spread yogurt mixture on bread slices. Arrange lettuce leaves on top of spread. Place turkey slices on lettuce. Place 3 or 4 orange slices down middle of each sandwich, overlapping slices. Drop a scant 1 teaspoon whole-cranberry sauce in the middle of each sandwich. Sprinkle remaining grated orange peel over sauce and turkey. Makes 4 servings.

Garden-Vegetable Chowder

Instant-potato flakes help make a quick, thick and rich-tasting chowder.

1/2 cup chopped onion
1 (16-oz.) pkg. frozen mixed vegetables,
  broken apart
1/4 teaspoon dried leaf thyme
1/2 teaspoon salt

3 cups Chicken Broth, page 16, or
  1-1/2 (14-1/2-oz.) cans regular-strength
  chicken broth
1 cup instant-potato flakes
1 cup low-fat milk

In a 3-quart saucepan, combine onion, mixed vegetables, thyme, salt and broth. Bring to a boil; reduce heat. Cover and simmer 15 minutes. Add potato flakes and milk. Stir vigorously with a fork until combined. Simmer 5 minutes longer, stirring occasionally. Ladle hot soup into individual bowls. Makes 6 (1-cup) servings.

Sherried Mushroom Soup

For a light supper, serve with a crunchy spinach salad.

8 oz. fresh mushrooms
1/4 cup chopped onion
1 garlic clove, minced
1 (10-1/2-oz.) can concentrated beef broth
1 cup water

1 tablespoon butter or margarine
2 green onions, sliced
2 tablespoons all-purpose flour
1 cup low-fat milk
2 tablespoons dry sherry

Set aside 6 mushrooms; coarsely chop remaining mushrooms, including stems. In a 3-quart saucepan, combine chopped mushrooms, onion, garlic, broth and water. Bring to a boil; reduce heat. Cover and simmer 15 minutes. Strain cooking liquid into a bowl, reserving mushroom mixture. Place mushroom mixture in a blender or food processor with 1 cup cooking liquid. Process until smooth; set aside. Slice reserved 6 mushrooms. Melt butter or margarine in the same saucepan. Add sliced mushrooms and green onions; sauté over medium heat 1 minute. Sprinkle flour over sautéed mixture. Stir until blended. Gradually add remaining cooking liquid, stirring constantly. Add milk and pureed mushroom mixture. Stir over medium heat until mixture thickens. Add sherry. Ladle hot soup into individual bowls. Makes 4 (1-cup) servings.

Chill bowls or stemmed glasses for serving cold soups.

Tuna-Rice Towers

Rice cakes are available in the Oriental sections of supermarkets and health-food stores.

1 cup plus 2 tablespoons part-skim ricotta cheese (9 oz.)	1 (6-1/2-oz.) can water-packed tuna, drained
4 rice cakes	1 green onion, sliced
2 tablespoons buttermilk or low-fat milk	2 teaspoons red-wine vinegar
1/4 teaspoon paprika	4 cherry tomatoes
8 pimiento-stuffed olives, thinly sliced	

Spread 1/4 cup ricotta cheese over each rice cake. In a small bowl, combine remaining 2 tablespoons ricotta cheese, buttermilk or low-fat milk and paprika. Stir until smooth; set aside. Arrange olive slices on cheese in a circle around edge of each rice cake. In a small bowl, break tuna into chunks with a fork. Add green onion. Sprinkle vinegar over tuna; toss gently with a fork. Pile tuna mixture on rice cakes inside olive ring. Spoon a dollop of reserved cheese mixture over tuna. Place 1 cherry tomato on top of each sandwich. Serve immediately. Makes 4 servings.

Gelled Mediterranean Bouillon

A soft gel that quickly melts in your mouth is a refreshing change from hot soup.

1 tablespoon olive oil	1 tablespoon lemon juice
1/2 cup chopped onion	1/8 teaspoon pepper
1/2 cup chopped green bell pepper	1 (.25-oz.) envelope unflavored gelatin
1 garlic clove, minced	1/4 cup cold water
1 small zucchini	1/3 cup plain yogurt
1 tomato, peeled, diced	1 tablespoon mayonnaise
1 tablespoon chopped fresh parsley	1 teaspoon chopped chives or green onion
1 (12-oz.) can tomato juice	1/4 teaspoon Beau Monde or
1 (10-1/2-oz.) can concentrated chicken broth	Bon Appétit seasoning

In a heavy 4-quart pot, heat oil. Add onion, green pepper and garlic. Sauté over medium-high heat until onion is tender. Grate zucchini without peeling. Add zucchini, tomato and parsley to onion mixture. Pour tomato juice and broth over vegetable mixture. Stir in lemon juice and pepper. Cover and simmer 10 minutes. In a small bowl, sprinkle gelatin over cold water. Let stand 3 to 4 minutes to soften. Remove soup from heat. Stir gelatin mixture into soup. Pour soup into a 2-quart container or casserole with a lid. Cover and refrigerate until gelled, at least 3 hours. In a small bowl, combine yogurt, mayonnaise, chives or green onion and Beau Monde or Bon Appétit seasoning. Refrigerate until needed. To serve, break up soup with a fork. Spoon into chilled cups or bowls. Top with a spoonful of seasoned yogurt. Makes 4 (1-cup) servings.

Tofu-Noodle Soup

Marinating tofu before adding to the soup gives it a lively flavor.

1 qt. Ginger-Chicken Broth, page 16; or
   2 (14-1/2-oz.) cans regular-strength
   chicken broth and 1/2 teaspoon
   grated fresh gingerroot
Tofu Marinade, see below
8 oz. tofu (bean curd), cut in
   1/2-inch cubes
2 tablespoons vegetable oil

1 small onion, sliced
8 fresh mushrooms, thinly sliced
1/2 medium zucchini, thinly sliced
1/2 small red or green bell pepper, diced
2 tablespoons cornstarch
1/4 cup cold water
1-1/2 cups chow mein noodles

Tofu Marinade:
1/4 cup soy sauce
1/2 cup water
2 tablespoons brown sugar

1 garlic clove, minced
2 teaspoons dry sherry
1 teaspoon honey

Prepare Ginger-Chicken Broth. Or, in a medium saucepan, combine broth and gingerroot. Cover and simmer 30 minutes. Strain broth, discarding gingerroot; keep hot. Prepare Tofu Marinade. Place tofu in an 8-inch-square baking pan. Pour marinade over tofu. Let stand 15 minutes, turning tofu once. Heat 1 tablespoon oil in a large skillet. Add onion and mushrooms; sauté over medium-high heat 1 minute. Add onion mixture to broth. Heat remaining 1 tablespoon oil in skillet. Add zucchini and red or green pepper. Cook 1 minute. Add to chicken broth. Lift tofu from marinade; add to broth. Stir 2 tablespoons marinade into broth. Cover and simmer 5 minutes. In a small bowl, combine cornstarch and cold water; stir until smooth. Pour cornstarch mixture in a thin stream into soup, stirring constantly. Bring soup to a boil, stirring constantly. Ladle hot soup into individual bowls. Sprinkle 1/4 cup chow mein noodles over each serving. Makes 6 (1-cup) servings.

Tofu Marinade:
Combine all ingredients in a small bowl. Set aside until ready to use.

Curried Fruit & Nuts

Tofu is high in protein and low in fat and calories!

8 oz. tofu (bean curd), drained
1/2 cup lemon-flavored yogurt
1/2 teaspoon curry powder
1 (16-oz.) can water-packed peach slices,
   drained
1/4 cup raisins

2 tablespoons unsweetened shredded coconut
2 tablespoons sliced almonds
4 leaves curly endive or other leaf lettuce
4 slices Poppy-Seed Egg Braid, page 36,
   or other egg bread

In a medium bowl, break up tofu with a fork or pastry blender until crumbly. Stir in yogurt and curry powder. Add peach slices, raisins, coconut and almonds. Stir gently to combine. Arrange endive or lettuce on bread slices. Spoon tofu mixture over endive or lettuce. Serve immediately. Makes 4 servings.

Shrimp & Egg Ranchero Stacks

Jícama is a crisp, potato-like Mexican vegetable, usually eaten raw.

Ranchero Sauce, see below
8 (1/4-inch) slices peeled jícama or
   4 slices Italian bread,
   cut in halves

2 cups shredded lettuce
4 hard-cooked eggs, sliced
8 medium, deveined, shelled cooked shrimp
8 pimiento-stuffed olives

Ranchero Sauce:
1 medium tomato, peeled, diced
1 (8-oz.) can tomato sauce
1 green onion, sliced
1/2 cup chopped green bell pepper

2 tablespoons fresh or
   canned diced green chilies
1/8 teaspoon salt

Prepare Ranchero Sauce. Refrigerate at least 1 hour. Place 4 slices jícama or 4 half-slices bread on a board or plate. Arrange 1/2 cup shredded lettuce on each slice. Drizzle Ranchero Sauce over lettuce. Overlap egg slices in a row the length of the jícama or bread slices. Place 2 shrimp diagonally across the row of egg on each sandwich. Drizzle more sauce over sandwiches. Top each with remaining jícama or bread. Place a wooden pick through each olive. Insert 2 wooden picks into the top of each sandwich. Makes 4 servings.

Ranchero Sauce:
Combine all ingredients in a small bowl. Stir until well blended. Set aside until ready to use.

Cheese & Popcorn Soup

A small amount of extra-sharp Cheddar cheese will give a good cheesy flavor.

1 teaspoon vegetable oil
1/4 cup chopped onion
1/4 cup sliced carrot
1/4 cup chopped celery
1 small tomato, peeled, diced
2 cups Chicken Broth, page 16, or
   1 (14-1/2-oz.) can regular-strength
   chicken broth

4 oz. Neufchâtel cheese, diced
1 teaspoon Champagne Mustard, page 40,
   or Dijon-style mustard
1 cup low-fat milk
1/2 cup shredded extra-sharp Cheddar
   cheese (2 oz.)
2 cups popped popcorn

In a small skillet, heat oil. Add onion, carrot and celery. Sauté over medium-high heat until vegetables are lightly coated with oil, about 30 seconds. Add tomato; cook 2 minutes longer. Combine sautéed vegetables and broth in a medium saucepan. Bring to a boil; reduce heat to low. Cover and simmer 20 minutes. Pour vegetable mixture into a blender or food processor. Add Neufchâtel cheese and mustard; process until smooth. Return pureed mixture to saucepan. Add milk and cheese. Stir over medium heat until cheese melts. Ladle hot soup into individual bowls. Sprinkle popcorn over each serving. Makes 4 (1-cup) servings.

How to Make Shrimp & Egg Ranchero Stacks

1/Peel off thick brown skin from jicama.

2/Garnish completed sandwiches with olives.

Tuna-Cheese Leaves

Curly, mild-flavored Savoy cabbage makes an excellent base for a sandwich.

1 (6-1/2-oz.) can water-packed tuna, drained
2 hard-cooked eggs
2 green onions, sliced
2 tablespoons oil-type Italian salad dressing

1 cup low-fat cottage cheese (8 oz.)
2 tablespoons sliced black olives
6 Savoy-cabbage leaves or loose-leaf lettuce

Place tuna in a medium bowl; break up with a fork. Finely chop eggs or force eggs through a sieve. Add chopped or sieved eggs, green onions and Italian dressing to tuna; stir to combine. Stir in cottage cheese and olives. Place 1 cabbage or lettuce leaf on each of 3 salad plates. Top cabbage or lettuce leaves with tuna mixture. Place remaining cabbage or lettuce leaves over tuna mixture. Serve sandwiches with knives and forks. Makes 3 servings.

Garden-Picked Pockets

Crunchy, fresh vegetables are satisfying to eat and nutritious too!

Vinaigrette Dressing, see below
1 small zucchini, thinly sliced
1 large carrot, shredded
1 cup cooked fresh or frozen green peas
10 cherry tomatoes, cut in halves

1 cup alfalfa sprouts
1 cup packed fresh spinach leaves
6 oz. Swiss cheese, diced
4 whole-wheat pita-bread rounds

Vinaigrette Dressing:
2 tablespoons vegetable oil
1 tablespoon olive oil
2 tablespoons lemon juice
1/4 teaspoon salt

Pinch of pepper
1 tablespoon chopped fresh parsley
1 garlic clove

Prepare Vinaigrette Dressing. In a medium bowl, combine zucchini, carrot, peas, tomatoes and sprouts. Using a sharp knife, shred spinach. Add shredded spinach and cheese to vegetables; toss until combined. Remove garlic from Vinaigrette Dressing. Pour dressing over vegetables; toss. Cover bowl and refrigerate until needed, up to 1 hour. Preheat oven to 250F (120C). Wrap bread rounds in foil. Heat in oven 15 minutes. Cut each bread round in half. Stuff both halves with vegetable mixture. Arrange 2 pockets on each plate. Makes 4 servings.

Vinaigrette Dressing:
In a small jar or airtight container, combine vegetable oil, olive oil, lemon juice, salt, pepper and parsley. Shake vigorously 1 minute. Crush garlic with flat side of a knife, keeping garlic in 1 piece. Add to dressing. Store in refrigerator until needed.

Ham & Melon Triangles

Neufchâtel cheese has fewer calories per ounce than cream cheese.

4 slices Russian Black Bread, page 43,
   or other black rye bread
2 (1-oz.) square slices sandwich ham
3 oz. Neufchâtel cheese, room temperature
1/4 teaspoon grated lemon peel

2 teaspoons lemon juice
1/4 teaspoon coarsely ground black pepper
1/4 medium cantaloupe
1/4 medium honeydew melon

Cut bread slices into squares the same size as ham slices. Cut ham slices in half diagonally. In a small bowl, combine cheese, lemon peel, lemon juice and pepper. Beat with an electric mixer until smooth. Spread cheese mixture evenly over bread squares. Place a ham triangle on each bread slice, matching corners. Cut cantaloupe and honeydew melon in 4 slices each. Peel melon slices. Arrange 1 cantaloupe slice and 1 honeydew slice diagonally across both ham and cheese triangles. Overlap melon slices at corner of cheese triangle. Makes 4 servings.

Sunday-Night Suppers

upper refers to the evening meal when the main meal is served at midday. After a heavy Sunday lunch, a sandwich or soup supper is just right. But any day of the week can be the perfect time. When mealtime is rushed or a casual, fun-to-eat supper will lighten spirits, soups or sandwiches are the answer.

Soups are often *better* the second day. Flavors have time to blend and the resulting combined taste develops. For a Sunday-night supper, soup can be prepared Saturday afternoon. For a supper during the work week, soup can be prepared on the weekend and stored several days. Leftover soup makes an easy supper. Combine leftover soup with a sandwich to make it a different meal.

All the sandwiches and soups in this chapter are hearty and filling. With a salad or light dessert, they make a hot meal that's warming and fun to eat. Mediterranean Meatball Soup is a complete meal in itself. With cheese-stuffed meatballs, pasta and vegetables in a flavorful garlic broth, all it needs is garlic toast and a refreshing sherbet dessert.

Hawaiian Ham Burgers are unique burgers that can be a sunny delight year round. The patties are made of ham and smothered with sweet and sour sauce. Pan-fry or broil the patties and stuff in pocket bread with orange slices, pineapple, lettuce and almonds. Complete the meal with fresh steamed broccoli and a twist of lemon.

Serve Chilly-Day Chili with a salad for a delicious supper. The menu below will give you more ideas. 🌺

Menu

Southwestern Flair

Old Pueblo Chicken Soup, page 110
Pear, Orange & Banana Slices on Spinach Leaves
Lemon-Yogurt Dressing
Squaw Bread, page 42

Teenagers' Favorite

Pepperoni Pitas, page 84
Cherry-Tomato, Mushroom, Green-Bean & Black-Olive Salad
Italian Dressing
Cherry-Macaroon Layers, page 146

Border Specials

America's Southwestern flavor in a triple-decker sandwich that oozes melted cheese.

12 slices Honey-Wheat-Nugget Bread,
   page 54, or other whole-wheat bread
1/4 cup Festive Chili Butter, page 39,
   butter or margarine, room temperature
4 oz. sliced roast beef
1 (4-oz.) can whole green chilies, drained

6 oz. Monterey Jack cheese, sliced
1 egg
2 tablespoons milk
1/8 teaspoon salt
2 tablespoons butter or margarine

Arrange 8 slices of bread on a work surface. Spread 1 side of each slice with Festive Chili Butter, butter or margarine. Place a layer of roast beef on each of 4 slices, making sure it does not extend beyond the bread. Cut chilies in half lengthwise; remove seeds. Cut chilies in 1/4-inch-wide strips. Arrange strips on beef-covered bread slices. Layer cheese on top of the other 4 buttered bread slices. Butter remaining 4 slices bread with Festive Chili Butter, butter or margarine. Place on chili strips, buttered-side up. Place cheese-topped bread slices on top, cheese-side down. Beat egg in a pie plate with a fork. Stir in milk and salt. Melt 1 tablespoon butter or margarine in a large skillet over medium-low heat. Dip top and bottom of 2 sandwiches in egg mixture; do not dip sides. Cook sandwiches in skillet until lightly browned on both sides. Keep sandwiches hot in a warm oven. Repeat with remaining 2 sandwiches, using remaining butter or margarine. Cut each sandwich in half. Serve hot. Makes 4 servings.

How to Make Border Specials

1/Arrange chilies on beef-covered slices. Place remaining buttered slices, butter-side up, over chilies. Finish sandwiches by topping with cheese-covered bread.

2/Dip top and bottom of 2 sandwiches at a time in egg mixture. Cook sandwiches until lightly browned on both sides.

Chilly-Day Chili

Use canned chili beans for a quick supper.

Corn Cakes, page 27, if desired
3 cups Chili Beans, see below, or
  2 (16-oz.) cans chili beans
1 lb. ground beef
1 cup chopped onion
1 cup chopped celery
2 garlic cloves, minced

3 tablespoons all-purpose flour
2 tablespoons chili powder
2 teaspoons salt
1 (12-oz.) can tomato juice
1 (10-1/2-oz.) can concentrated beef broth
1 (28-oz.) can whole tomatoes

Chili Beans:
1-1/2 cups dried pinto beans or red beans
3 cups water
1 teaspoon salt
1 tablespoon vegetable oil

1/2 cup chopped onion
1 tablespoon chili powder
2 tablespoons taco sauce

Prepare Corn Cakes, if desired. Prepare Chili Beans, if using, or heat canned beans and keep warm. Brown ground beef in a large skillet until no longer pink. Drain all but 2 tablespoons drippings from skillet. Add onion, celery and garlic to beef and 2 tablespoons drippings. Sauté until onion is tender. In a small bowl, combine flour, chili powder and salt. Sprinkle flour mixture over browned beef; stir to coat. Gradually stir in tomato juice and beef broth. Pour beef mixture into warm beans. Chop tomatoes. Stir chopped tomatoes with liquid into beef mixture. Bring to a boil. Reduce heat. Cover and simmer 15 minutes. Ladle hot soup into individual bowls. Serve with Corn Cakes to float on top, if desired. Makes 6 (2-cup) servings.

Chili Beans:
Sort and rinse beans. Place beans in a large saucepan. Cover with water to about 3 inches above beans. Soak 8 hours or overnight. Or, quick-soak by bringing beans and water to a boil. Boil 2 minutes; remove from heat. Cover and let stand 1 hour. Drain soaked beans, discarding water. Combine soaked beans, 3 cups water and salt in large saucepan. In a small skillet, heat oil. Add onion; sauté until tender. Stir chili powder and taco sauce into onion. Pour onion mixture into beans. Bring to a boil; reduce heat. Cover and simmer until beans are tender, 1 to 1-1/2 hours. Add hot water, if necessary, to keep beans covered during cooking. Keep warm until ready to use.

Old Pueblo Chicken Soup

Cilantro is fresh coriander, a common ingredient in Mexican cooking.

1-1/2 lbs. meaty chicken pieces
6 cups water
4 chicken bouillon cubes
1 medium onion, cut in quarters
1 carrot, sliced
1 celery stalk including leafy top, sliced
1 bay leaf
1 tablespoon chopped fresh parsley
1/2 teaspoon salt

1 medium, green bell pepper
1/2 lb. fresh tomatillos or
   1 (12-oz.) can tomatillos
1 medium onion, thinly sliced
1 (15-1/2-oz.) can garbanzo beans, drained
1 (4-oz.) can diced green chilies, drained
1/4 cup fresh cilantro leaves
6 oz. Monterey Jack cheese
1 avocado

Place chicken pieces in a 6-quart pot. Add water, bouillon cubes, quartered onion, carrot, celery, bay leaf, parsley and salt. Bring to a boil. Skim foam from surface until surface is clear. Cover and simmer until chicken is tender, about 30 minutes. Remove chicken; set aside to cool. Line a sieve with cheesecloth. Strain cooking liquid through sieve into a large bowl. Discard vegetables and herbs. Spoon fat from surface of liquid. Pull strips of paper towel across surface of liquid to remove any fat. Rinse pot. Return cooking liquid to pot. Cut green pepper in 2'' x 1/4'' strips. Peel fresh tomatillos; slice crosswise. If using canned tomatillos, drain and cut in half crosswise. Add onion slices, pepper strips, tomatillos, garbanzo beans, green chilies and cilantro to cooking liquid. Remove skin from cooked chicken. Pull meat from bones. Discard skin and bones. Cut meat in 1/2-inch cubes. Add cooked chicken to pot. Cover and simmer 20 minutes. Cut cheese in 1/2-inch cubes. To serve, ladle hot soup into individual bowls. Scatter 5 or 6 cheese cubes in each bowl. Thinly slice avocado; float 3 or 4 slices in each bowl. Makes 6 (2-cup) servings.

Thanksgiving-Turkey Soup

Simmer the leftover holiday bird for the best-tasting, easiest homemade soup ever!

1 turkey carcass
1 medium onion, sliced
1 celery stalk including leafy top, sliced
10 cups water
2 bay leaves
1/2 teaspoon dried leaf thyme

8 black peppercorns
2 teaspoons salt
Basil & Cheese Dumplings, page 22
1/2 lb. fresh broccoli or
   1 (9-oz.) pkg. frozen chopped broccoli
2 cups packed fresh spinach leaves

Break turkey carcass into pieces. Place in a 6- to 8-quart pot. Add onion, celery and water. Bring to a boil. Reduce heat to maintain a gentle boil. Skim foam from surface until surface is clear. Add bay leaves, thyme, peppercorns and salt. Simmer, with lid ajar, 6 hours. Remove turkey bones; discard. Strain liquid through a colander into a large container. Rinse pot with water. Line a sieve with cheesecloth. Strain cooking liquid back into clean pot through cheesecloth-lined sieve. Discard vegetables and herbs. Set cooking liquid aside 20 minutes to allow fat to come to the surface. Prepare batter for Basil & Cheese Dumplings. Skim fat from liquid; discard. Stir broccoli and spinach into liquid; return to heat. Bring to a boil. Reduce heat and simmer. Drop rounded teaspoonfuls of Basil & Cheese-Dumpling batter into simmering liquid. Cover and simmer until dumplings are firm, about 15 minutes. Ladle hot soup into individual bowls, placing 3 dumplings in each serving. Makes 6 (1-1/2-cup) servings.

Mushroom-Barley Soup

Thick like a porridge, with a distinct mushroom flavor.

6 oz. fresh mushrooms
3 tablespoons butter or margarine
1 garlic clove, minced
1 teaspoon dried marjoram
1-3/4 cups Beef Broth, page 14, or
   1 (14-1/2-oz.) can regular-strength
   beef broth
3-1/2 cups water

1/2 teaspoon salt
1/8 teaspoon black pepper
1 bay leaf
1/2 lb. ground beef
1 lb. potatoes, peeled, cut in 3/4-inch cubes
3/4 cup barley
2 cups packed fresh spinach leaves
1 cup milk

Wipe mushrooms with a damp cloth. Set aside 2 mushrooms; chop remaining mushrooms. Melt butter or margarine in a 4-quart pot. Add chopped mushrooms and garlic. Cook, stirring, over medium-high heat, until mushrooms darken. Sprinkle marjoram over cooked mushrooms. Add broth, water, salt, pepper and bay leaf. Brown ground beef in a medium skillet until no longer pink. Drain off drippings. Add browned beef, potato cubes and barley to pot; bring to a boil. Reduce heat. Cover and simmer until potatoes and barley are tender, about 30 minutes. Discard bay leaf. Cut spinach leaves in strips. Stir spinach and milk into pot. Cover and cook 5 minutes longer. Do not boil. Slice reserved mushrooms. Ladle hot soup into individual bowls. Float a mushroom slice on top of each serving. Makes 6 (2-cup) servings.

Taste O'Roma

You'll need a knife and fork for this open-face sausage-and-pepper sandwich.

1 lb. Italian sausage
1 (15-oz.) can tomato sauce
1/2 teaspoon dried leaf oregano
1 medium, green bell pepper
1 medium, red bell pepper
2 tablespoons olive oil
1 medium, red onion, sliced
2 tablespoons butter or margarine,
   room temperature

1 small garlic clove, minced
4 slices Italian bread
1 (6-oz.) jar marinated artichoke hearts,
   drained
12 pitted black olives
1 cup shredded provolone or
   mozzarella cheese (4 oz.)

Cut sausage into 1-inch pieces. Brown in a large skillet until no longer pink. Using a slotted spoon, place sausage in a medium saucepan; discard drippings. Add tomato sauce and oregano. Cover and simmer 15 minutes. Cut green and red peppers in 2'' x 1/4'' strips. In a large skillet, heat oil. Add onion and pepper strips. Sauté over medium-high heat until onion is tender. Add onion mixture to sausage mixture. Combine butter or margarine and garlic in a small bowl. Preheat broiler. Place bread slices on a baking sheet. Spread garlic mixture on 1 side of each slice. Toast bread, buttered-side up, under broiler until lightly browned. Arrange artichoke hearts and olives on toasted bread. Spoon sausage mixture over top. Sprinkle cheese over sausage. Broil until cheese melts. Serve hot. Makes 4 servings.

Hawaiian Ham Burgers

Ask the butcher to grind pork for you. Do not use seasoned pork sausage.

1 (6-3/4-oz.) can chunk ham
1 lb. fresh ground pork
1/8 teaspoon pepper
1 slice bread
1 egg, beaten

Sweet & Sour Sauce, see below
2 fresh oranges
6 pita-bread rounds
2 cups shredded lettuce
1/2 cup sliced almonds, if desired

Sweet & Sour Sauce:
1 (8-oz.) can pineapple tidbits
Water
1-1/2 tablespoons soy sauce
3 tablespoons cider vinegar
6 tablespoons brown sugar

2 tablespoons cornstarch
1 green onion, sliced
1/4 cup diced red or green bell pepper
Hot-pepper sauce, if desired

Finely chop ham. Combine chopped ham, ground pork and pepper in a medium bowl. Break bread in pieces. Place in a blender or food processor. Process to uniform crumbs. Add bread-crumbs and egg to ham mixture; blend well. Shape ham mixture into 6 (1/2-inch-thick) patties. Prepare Sweet & Sour Sauce. Pan-fry ham patties in a large skillet, or broil patties about 5 minutes on each side. Be sure patties are well done. Remove peel from oranges, leaving no white pith. Slice oranges crosswise. Cut a 1-inch slice off 1 side of each bread round. Save slice for a snack. Open each bread round. Spoon some Sweet & Sour Sauce into each pocket. Place a ham patty in each pocket. Surround ham patty with orange slices and lettuce. Spoon more sauce into sandwiches. Sprinkle with almonds, if desired. Makes 6 servings.

Sweet & Sour Sauce:
Drain pineapple, reserving juice. Measure juice; add water to make 1 cup. Pour juice into a small saucepan. Add soy sauce, vinegar, brown sugar and cornstarch. Stir until sugar dissolves. Bring to a boil, stirring constantly. Continue cooking until thickened and smooth. Add drained pineapple, green onion and red or green pepper. Season to taste with hot-pepper sauce, if desired. Keep warm until ready to serve.

Wrap bread for freezing in foil or freezer wrap. Do not use the plastic bags from store-bought bread. They will not prevent moisture loss.

Hawaiian Ham Burger

Mediterranean Meatball Soup

Use turmeric instead of saffron to get a similar yellow-orange color.

2 qts. Chicken Broth, page 16, or
    4-1/2 (14-1/2-oz.) cans regular-
    strength chicken broth
1 tablespoon olive oil
2 garlic cloves, minced
1/2 cup chopped onion
1/2 cup sliced celery
2 medium tomatoes
1 tablespoon chopped fresh parsley or
    1 teaspoon dried leaf parsley

1 bay leaf
1 teaspoon dried leaf oregano
1/2 teaspoon dried leaf basil
1/4 teaspoon dried leaf thyme
1/4 teaspoon saffron threads or
    1/2 teaspoon ground turmeric
Mozzarella Meatballs, see below
1/2 cup pasta bows

Mozzarella Meatballs:
3/4 lb. ground beef
1/4 lb. ground pork
1 slice bread
1 teaspoon salt

1 teaspoon dried leaf basil
1/8 teaspoon pepper
1 egg, slightly beaten
4 oz. mozzarella cheese, cut in 16 cubes

In a medium saucepan, bring broth to a boil. Keep warm over low heat. Heat olive oil in a medium skillet. Add garlic, onion and celery. Sauté over medium-high heat until onion is tender. Place tomatoes in boiling water for 30 seconds. Lift from water and immediately plunge in cold water. Slip off skins. Cut tomatoes in 1-inch cubes. Add to sautéed vegetables. Cover and cook over medium heat 5 minutes. Add vegetable mixture to broth. In a cheesecloth bag, tie together parsley, bay leaf, oregano, basil and thyme. Add spice bag to broth. Stir in saffron or turmeric. Cover and simmer 30 minutes. Prepare Mozzarella Meatballs. Add meatballs and pasta to soup. Simmer until pasta is tender, 10 to 12 minutes. Ladle hot soup into individual bowls with 3 or 4 meatballs in each serving. Makes 6 (1-1/2-cup) servings.

Mozzarella Meatballs:

Combine ground beef and pork in a medium bowl. Break bread in pieces. Place in a blender or food processor. Process to uniform crumbs. Add breadcrumbs, salt, basil and pepper to meat mixture. Blend well. Add egg; blend well. Flatten about 1 tablespoon meat mixture in palm of your hand. Place 1 cheese cube in center of meat in your hand. Form meatball around cheese. Repeat with remaining meat mixture and cheese cubes, making 16 meatballs. Brown meatballs in a medium skillet until no longer pink. Set aside until ready to use.

Always add clams to the chowder at the last minute and cook just until heated through. If overcooked, clams become tough.

Manhattan-Style Clam Chowder

Sometimes called red clam chowder because of its tomato-clam-juice broth.

36 hard-shell or littleneck clams, or
  2 (7-1/2-oz.) cans minced clams and
  1 (12-oz.) bottle clam juice
2 cups water
3 bacon slices, diced
1 cup chopped onion
1 cup sliced celery
1/2 cup chopped carrot

2 cups diced potatoes (about 2 medium)
1 (28-oz.) can whole tomatoes, drained,
  chopped
1 cup water
1 bay leaf
1/2 teaspoon dried leaf thyme
Salt and freshly ground black pepper
  to taste

Rinse fresh clams. Place fresh clams and 2 cups water in a 4-quart pot; bring to a boil. Cover and cook until clam shells open, about 10 minutes. Discard any clams that do not open. Drain clams, reserving cooking liquid. Remove and discard clam shells. Chop clams; set aside. If using canned clams, drain, reserving liquid. Add clam juice to reserved liquid to make 2 cups. Rinse and dry 4-quart pot. Fry bacon until crisp in 4-quart pot. Remove bacon from pot using a slotted spoon, reserving drippings. Drain bacon on paper towels. Add onion, celery and carrot to bacon drippings; sauté over medium-high heat until onion is tender. Add diced pototoes, reserved clam cooking liquid, tomatoes, 1 cup water, bay leaf and thyme. Cover and simmer until potatoes are tender, about 35 minutes. Discard bay leaf. Stir in clams. Season to taste with salt and pepper. Ladle hot chowder into individual bowls. Sprinkle cooked bacon pieces over each serving. Makes 6 (1-1/2-cup) servings.

Creamy Clam Chowder

Thick, cream-colored chowder New Englanders claim as the original.

36 hard-shell or littleneck clams; or
  2 (7-1/2-oz.) cans minced clams and
  1 (12-oz.) bottle clam juice
2 cups water
3 bacon slices, diced
1 cup chopped onion
1 cup sliced celery

4 cups diced potatoes (about 4 medium)
2 cups milk
1 cup half and half
Salt to taste
2 to 4 tablespoons instant-potato flakes
Freshly ground black pepper
2 tablespoons butter

Rinse fresh clams. Place fresh clams and 2 cups water in a 4-quart pot; bring to a boil. Cover and cook until clam shells open, about 10 minutes. Discard any clams that do not open. Drain clams, reserving cooking liquid. Remove and discard clam shells. Chop clams; set aside. If using canned clams, drain, reserving liquid. Add clam juice to reserved liquid to make 2 cups. Rinse and dry 4-quart pot. Fry bacon until crisp in 4-quart pot. Remove bacon from pot using a slotted spoon, reserving drippings. Drain bacon on paper towels. Add onion and celery to bacon drippings. Sauté over medium-high heat until onion is tender. Add diced potatoes and reserved clam cooking liquid. Cover and simmer until potatoes are tender, about 20 minutes. Remove 1 cup diced potatoes. Puree in a blender or food processor with milk and half and half. Pour potato puree into pot in a thin stream while stirring. Season to taste with salt. Add potato flakes, 2 tablespoons at a time, stirring between additions until chowder reaches desired consistency. Add clams and reserved cooked bacon. Simmer until heated through, 8 to 10 minutes. Do not boil. Ladle hot chowder into individual bowls. Sprinkle each bowl with pepper and top with 1 teaspoon butter. Makes 6 (1-1/2-cup) servings.

Corn-on-the-Cob Soup

At its best when fresh corn is available.

1 tablespoon vegetable oil
1 lb. boneless pork, cut in
    2" x 1/4" strips
1 cup chopped onion
1 garlic clove, minced
1 qt. Chicken Broth, page 16, or
    2 (14-1/2-oz.) cans regular-strength
    chicken broth
2 cups Beef Broth, page 14, or
    1 (14-1/2-oz.) can regular-
    strength beef broth

1 bay leaf
1/2 teaspoon salt
1/2 teaspoon dried leaf basil
1/8 teaspoon dried leaf thyme
6 ears sweet corn, fresh or frozen
2 medium tomatoes, peeled, diced
1 medium zucchini, thinly sliced

Heat oil in a large skillet over high heat 1 minute. Add pork strips; sauté until brown. Lift pork from skillet. Place in a 4-quart pot. Stir onion and garlic into pan drippings. Sauté until tender. Stir sautéed onion and garlic into pork. Add broths, bay leaf, salt, basil and thyme to pot. Bring to a boil; reduce heat. Cover and simmer 1 hour. Cut or break corn into 3- to 4-inch pieces. Add corn, tomatoes and zucchini to pot. Simmer 15 minutes longer. Ladle hot soup into individual bowls. Makes 6 (2-cup) servings.

Old-Fashioned Split-Pea with Ham Soup

Leeks may be omitted if they are not available.

1 lb. green split peas
2 qts. water
1 (1-lb.) meaty ham shank
2 leeks
2 tablespoons butter or margarine
1 celery stalk including leafy top, sliced
1/2 cup chopped onion

2 medium potatoes, peeled, diced
1 teaspoon salt
1/4 teaspoon white pepper
1 bay leaf
1 cup milk
Dairy sour cream
Poppy seeds, if desired

Sort and rinse peas; place in a 4-quart pot. Add water and ham shank. Wash leeks thoroughly. Trim, leaving 3 inches of green tops. Cut leeks into 1/4-inch slices. Melt butter or margarine in a skillet. Add leeks, celery and onion. Sauté over medium-high heat until tender. Add sautéed vegetables, potatoes, salt, white pepper and bay leaf to pot. Bring to a boil; reduce heat. Cover and simmer until peas are tender, about 45 minutes. Remove bay leaf and ham shank. Pull ham from bone; discard bone and bay leaf. Dice ham; set aside. Puree cooked pea mixture in a blender or food processor; return to pot. Stir in milk and diced ham. Cook over medium heat 10 minutes, stirring frequently to prevent scorching. Ladle hot soup into individual bowls. Top each serving with a dollop of sour cream. Sprinkle poppy seeds over sour cream, if desired. Makes 6 (2-cup) servings.

Corn-on-the-Cob Soup and Squaw Bread, page 42.

Pepper-Beef Slices

Bake sandwich loaf wrapped in foil for a softer crust.

Tangy-Sweet Spread, page 46,
   room temperature
1 lb. beef round steak or flank steak
1 tablespoon vegetable oil
1/2 cup coarsely chopped onion
1 teaspoon grated fresh gingerroot or
   1/2 teaspoon ground ginger
1/4 teaspoon pepper

1 (10-1/2-oz.) can concentrated beef broth
1 tablespoon soy sauce
1 medium, green bell pepper
1 tablespoon cornstarch
1/3 cup cold water
1 (1-lb.) loaf unsliced French or
   Italian bread

Prepare Tangy-Sweet Spread. Cut beef in 2" x 1/2" x 1/8" slivers. Heat oil in a large skillet. Add beef; sauté until no longer pink. Push beef to 1 side. Add onion and ginger to pan drippings. Sauté until onion is tender. Stir onion into beef; season with pepper. Stir in broth and soy sauce. Bring to a boil; reduce heat. Cover and simmer until beef is tender, about 45 minutes. Cut green pepper in 2" x 1/4" strips; add to beef mixture. Cover and simmer 5 minutes longer. Preheat oven to 350F (175C). Combine cornstarch and cold water in a small bowl. Gradually stir cornstarch mixture into beef mixture. Cook, stirring constantly, until thickened. Cut a 2-inch slice off each end of bread. Using a long knife, hollow out middle of loaf, cutting bread from both ends. Leave a 1-inch shell of bread all the way around. Use middle of bread for another purpose such as croutons or crumbs. Spread inside of bread shell with Tangy-Sweet Spread. Place end slice back on 1 end of loaf. Secure with wooden picks. Spoon hot filling into bread shell. Replace other end slice of bread. Secure with wooden picks. Place loaf on a baking sheet. Bake, uncovered, 10 minutes. To serve, cut in 1-1/2-inch slices. Lay each slice flat on individual plates. Makes 6 servings.

Classic Reuben

Serve with lots of paper napkins!

1 (16-oz.) can sauerkraut
1/2 cup beer
1/4 cup chopped onion
8 slices rye bread
3 tablespoons Savory Butter, page 36,
   butter or margarine, room temperature

1/2 lb. sliced corned beef
6 oz. sliced Swiss cheese
1/2 cup Special Hamburger Sauce, page 33,
   or Thousand Island dressing
Dill-pickle spears, if desired

In a medium saucepan, combine sauerkraut, beer and onion. Cover and simmer 15 minutes. Spread 1 side of each slice of bread with Savory Butter, butter or margarine. Prepare 2 sandwiches at a time as follows: On a griddle or large skillet, place 4 slices of bread, buttered-side down. Top 2 of the slices with half the corned beef and the other 2 with half the cheese. Grill bread until crisp and golden brown. Remove bread slices; place on a baking sheet. Keep hot in a warm oven. Repeat with remaining bread, corned beef and cheese. Spread Special Hamburger Sauce or Thousand Island dressing over corned-beef-covered bread slices. Using a slotted spoon, put a generous layer of sauerkraut mixture on top of each. Place cheese-covered bread slices on top of sauerkraut mixture, cheese-side down. Cut each sandwich in half. Serve with dill-pickle spears, if desired. Makes 4 servings.

How to Make Pepper-Beef Slices

1/Cut a 2-inch slice off each end of bread. Using a long knife, hollow out middle of loaf, cutting bread from both ends. Leave a 1-inch shell of bread.

2/Spread inside of bread shell with Tangy-Sweet Spread. Place end slice back on 1 end of loaf. Secure with wooden picks. Spoon hot filling into bread shell.

Double-Stuffed Hot Dogs

A hot dog and hamburger together in a bun.

1 lb. lean ground beef
1/2 cup fine fresh breadcrumbs
2 tablespoons chopped onion
2 tablespoons chopped green bell pepper
1 teaspoon Worcestershire sauce
1/2 teaspoon salt
1/2 cup smoky barbecue sauce

4 smoked sausage links or hot dogs
1 tablespoon butter or margarine
1 medium onion, sliced
4 Hot-Dog Buns, page 33,
    or other hot-dog buns
4 oz. Cheddar cheese, sliced

Preheat oven to 350F (175C). In a medium bowl, combine ground beef, breadcrumbs, onion, green pepper, Worcestershire sauce, salt and 2 tablespoons barbecue sauce. Divide meat mixture into 4 parts. Shape each portion around a sausage or hot dog, covering it completely. Place on a 15'' x 10'' jelly-roll pan. Bake 20 minutes. Heat butter or margarine in a large skillet. Add onion; sauté until tender. Stir in remaining barbecue sauce; keep warm. Cut hot-dog buns lengthwise nearly in two. Open buns. Place buns, split-side up, on a baking sheet. Arrange cheese slices on open buns. Place buns in oven during last 2 minutes of cooking sausages or hot dogs. Place a cooked sausage or hot dog on each bun. Spoon warm onion mixture over top. Serve hot. Makes 4 servings.

Around the World

S oups and sandwiches are universal foods enjoyed around the world. As more of us travel, favorite international recipes are brought home. Many soups and sandwiches with French, Italian, Russian or Mexican names are served today and recognized by name.

Most countries have several soups that are unique to that country. These soups often feature meats and vegetables raised or grown and enjoyed in the area. Scotch Broth makes use of lamb, an animal raised in the Scottish Highlands. Beets are the essential ingredient in Russian Chlodnik. Spanish cooks often make use of spicy, garlicky sausages. Our hearty Caldo Gallego combines sausage with beans, potatoes and greens. Won-Ton Soup uses the Chinese vegetable *bok choy.*

Like the American hot dog, other countries have sandwiches that represent them. In many countries, street vendors sell their special sandwiches along the main streets of towns and cities. People walk the streets munching these fresh, hot treats. Many of these sandwiches are now popular outside their country of origin, not only in ethnic restaurants, but prepared at home.

The Middle Eastern Felafel sandwich is a vegetarian delight. Garbanzo-bean-and-sesame balls are stuffed in pocket bread. Lots of fresh vegetables and in our version, Cucumber-Yogurt Sauce, makes it a crunchy, fresh, good-for-you sandwich. Greek Gyro also starts with pocket bread. But instead of stuffing the pocket, the flat bread is wrapped around a spicy lamb filling. A napkin is wrapped around the sandwich to keep it rolled and catch the drips of Dilled Yogurt Sauce.

Calzone is an Italian antipasto wrapped in bread dough and baked. Like any good antipasto, salami, ham, cheese, mushrooms and olives are included. The sandwich is served pizza-style with a sprinkling of cheese and tomato sauce poured over the top.

Recipes in this chapter were not gathered from around-the-world travel, but were developed in our own kitchen using readily available ingredients. We hope they will give you a taste of many lands without leaving your own kitchen. ❧

Menu

Scandinavian Brunch

Tomato-Juice Cocktails
Open-Face Scandinavian Smørrebrød,
page 126
Butter-Pecan Cookies
Coffee, Tea

Greek Patio Lunch

Zucchini Avgolemono, page 127
Greek Gyro, page 125
Strawberry Ribbons, page 154
White-Wine Spritzers

Calzone

Much like pizza, these Italian turnovers can be eaten out of hand or with a knife and fork.

Calzone Dough, see below
1/4 cup Italian oil-type salad dressing
2 cups shredded mozzarella cheese (8 oz.)
4 oz. salami, cut in slivers
4 oz. ham, cut in slivers
1/3 cup sliced black olives
1 (2-oz.) can mushroom pieces, drained
2 (8-oz.) cans tomato sauce
1 garlic clove, minced

1/4 teaspoon salt
1/4 teaspoon dried leaf oregano
1/4 teaspoon dried leaf basil
Pinch of sugar
1 tablespoon butter or margarine, melted
6 tablespoons freshly grated Parmesan cheese
 (1-1/4 oz.)

Calzone Dough:
1 cup warm water (105F, 40C)
1 (1/4-oz.) pkg. active dry yeast
 (1 tablespoon)
1 teaspoon sugar

2 tablespoons vegetable oil
1 teaspoon salt
1-1/2 cups bread flour or all-purpose flour
1-1/2 to 2 cups all-purpose flour

Prepare Calzone Dough; let rise. Punch down dough by pushing your fist into center; pull edges of dough over center. Turn out dough on a floured surface. Knead 5 times. Divide dough into 6 parts. Roll out each part to a 6-inch circle. Brush each circle with salad dressing. In a medium bowl, combine mozzarella cheese, salami, ham, olives and mushroom pieces; toss lightly. Place about 1/2 cup cheese mixture in center of each dough circle. Pull 2 opposite edges up over filling. Crimp edges as for pie crust. Cover with a towel. Let rise 15 minutes. Combine tomato sauce, garlic, salt, oregano, basil and sugar in a small saucepan. Cover and simmer 10 minutes. Preheat oven to 400F (205C). Bake 15 minutes. Brush each Calzone with melted butter or margarine and sprinkle with Parmesan cheese. Bake until golden brown, about 5 minutes longer. Serve hot. Pass tomato sauce separately for spooning over the top. Makes 6 servings.

Calzone Dough:
Pour warm water into a large bowl; stir in yeast and sugar until dissolved. Set aside until foamy, about 15 minutes. Add oil, salt and 1-1/2 cups bread flour or all-purpose flour; beat until smooth. Add remaining all-purpose flour, 1/2 cup at a time, until dough pulls away from side of bowl. Turn out on a lightly floured surface. Knead dough, adding flour as needed, until smooth and elastic, about 8 to 10 minutes. Clean and grease bowl. Place dough in bowl, turning to grease all sides. Cover with a dry cloth. Let rise in a warm place until dough has doubled in size, about 2 hours.

Won-Ton Soup

Egg-roll wrappers may be cut in quarters to make won-ton wrappers.

6 cups Ginger-Chicken Broth, page 16; or
   3 (14-1/2-oz.) cans regular-
   strength chicken broth and
   2 (1/4-inch) slices fresh gingerroot,
   peeled
Won-Ton Filling, see below

1 egg
1 tablespoon water
24 won-ton wrappers
4 stalks bok choy or Swiss chard,
   including leaves

Won-Ton Filling:
1 cup packed fresh spinach leaves
1/2 lb. lean ground pork
1 tablespoon soy sauce
1 teaspoon shredded peeled gingerroot

1 green onion, sliced
1/2 teaspoon salt
1/4 teaspoon black pepper

Prepare Ginger-Chicken Broth; or simmer canned broth with gingerroot, covered, 30 minutes. Strain broth, discarding gingerroot. Prepare Won-Ton Filling. In a small bowl, beat together egg and water. Place a won-ton wrapper on a work surface with 1 corner toward you. Spoon about 1 teaspoon filling in center of wrapper. Using your fingers, moisten 2 adjacent sides farthest from you with beaten egg. Fold corner close to you over filling to opposite corner, making a triangle. Press edges to seal. Moisten top surface of left corner of triangle and bottom surface of right corner. Taking triangle in the fingers of both hands, pull corners down under triangle. Overlap corners. Pinch ends together. Place finished won tons on a plate. Cover with a dry cloth. Fill remaining won-ton wrappers. Bring chicken broth to a boil in a large saucepan. Carefully slide won tons into broth. Return to a boil. Reduce heat to low; broth should simmer gently. Cook won tons until tender, about 5 minutes. Cut bok-choy or chard stems in diagonal slices. Cut leaves in shreds. Add to soup. Cover and simmer 5 minutes longer. Ladle 4 won tons into each bowl. Cover with broth and bok choy or chard. Makes 6 (1-1/2-cup) servings.

Won-Ton Filling:
Shred fresh spinach leaves with a knife. Steam spinach or boil in a small amount of water until tender; drain. Squeeze spinach to remove excess water. In a bowl, combine spinach and remaining ingredients. Set aside until ready to use.

How to Make Won-Ton Soup

1/Spoon filling in center of wrapper. Moisten sides farthest from you with beaten egg. Fold corner close to you over filling to opposite corner, making a triangle. Press edges to seal.

2/Moisten top surface of left corner of triangle and bottom surface of right corner. Taking triangle in fingers of both hands, pull corners down under triangle. Overlap corners. Pinch ends together.

Sopa Seca de Tortilla

Translated, this means Tortilla Dry Soup. Most of the soup liquid is absorbed by the tortillas.

12 (6-inch) corn tortillas
Oil for frying
1 tablespoon vegetable oil
1 cup chopped onion
1 garlic clove, minced
1/2 cup chopped green bell pepper
1 (16-oz.) can whole tomatoes
1/2 teaspoon salt

1/2 teaspoon dried leaf oregano
2 cups diced cooked chicken
2 cups shredded Monterey Jack cheese (8 oz.)
1 cup Chicken Broth, page 16, or
   canned regular-strength chicken broth
1/3 cup dairy sour cream
3 cilantro or parsley sprigs

Cut tortillas in 2" x 1/2" strips. Pour oil 1/2 inch deep in a heavy skillet. Heat oil to 350F (175C) or until a tortilla strip added to oil turns brown in 60 seconds. Add tortilla strips. Fry until lightly browned but not crisp. Drain on paper towels. In another skillet, heat 1 tablespoon oil. Add onion, garlic and green pepper. Sauté until onion is tender. Drain tomatoes, reserving liquid. Dice tomatoes. Add tomatoes, reserved liquid, salt and oregano to onion mixture. Stir well. Preheat oven to 375F (190C). Arrange 1/3 of tortilla strips on the bottom of a 2-quart casserole. Spoon about 1/3 tomato mixture over tortillas. Sprinkle 1/3 of chicken and cheese over the top. Repeat layering 2 more times. Bring broth to a boil. Pour around edges of casserole. Cover casserole and bake 15 minutes. Uncover and bake 15 minutes longer. Top with sour cream and sprigs of cilantro or parsley. Serve immediately. Makes 4 (1-1/2-cup) servings.

Albondigas

Cilantro or fresh coriander is a common seasoning in Mexican and Middle Eastern cooking.

2 qts. Chicken Broth, page 16, or
    4-1/2 (14-1/2-oz.) cans regular-
    strength chicken broth
1 (28-oz.) can whole tomatoes
1 tablespoon vegetable oil
1 cup chopped onion
1 garlic clove, minced
2 cups sliced carrots

1 (4-oz.) can diced green chilies
1 teaspoon chili powder
1/2 teaspoon dried leaf oregano
1 teaspoon salt
1/2 teaspoon pepper
2 tablespoons chopped fresh cilantro
Meatballs, see below

Meatballs:
1 slice white bread
1/4 cup milk
1 lb. lean ground beef
1/4 lb. ground pork
2 tablespoons uncooked white rice

2 tablespoons finely chopped onion
1-1/4 teaspoons salt
1 teaspoon ground cumin
1/2 teaspoon dried leaf oregano
1 egg, beaten

Heat broth in a large saucepan. Drain juice from tomatoes; add to hot broth. Dice tomatoes; add to broth. In a large skillet, heat oil. Add onion, garlic and carrot slices. Sauté until onion is tender. Add onion mixture, chilies, chili powder, oregano, salt, pepper and cilantro to broth. Bring to a boil; reduce heat. Prepare Meatballs; add to broth. Cover and simmer 15 minutes. Ladle hot soup into individual bowls, including 4 meatballs in each bowl. Makes 6 (2-cup) servings.

Meatballs:
Place bread in a mixing bowl. Pour milk over bread. Let soak 5 minutes. Add beef and pork to bowl; blend well. Add rice, onion, salt, cumin and oregano; blend well. Stir beaten egg into meat mixture until blended. Shape meat mixture into 24 walnut-size balls. Set aside until ready to use.

Meat and vegetables for broth are cut in pieces so more flavor will be released into the broth.

Greek Gyro

Fenugreek, an ingredient in curry powder, can be purchased in health-food stores or specialty shops.

Dilled Yogurt Sauce, page 53
1/2 lb. ground lamb
1/2 lb. ground beef
2 slices white bread
2 tablespoons chopped fresh parsley or
   2 teaspoons dried leaf parsley
1 garlic clove, minced
1 teaspoon salt

1/8 teaspoon pepper
1/4 teaspoon ground fenugreek
1/2 teaspoon ground cumin
1 egg, beaten
6 pita-bread rounds
6 green onions
12 Greek olives or black olives

Prepare Dilled Yogurt Sauce. Combine lamb and beef in a medium bowl. Break white-bread slices in pieces. Place in a blender or food processor. Process to uniform crumbs. Add breadcrumbs, parsley, garlic, salt, pepper, fenugreek and cumin to meat mixture. Blend well. Stir egg into meat mixture. Preheat oven to 375F (190C). Form meat mixture into 6 logs, each about 4 inches long. Place logs on a 15'' x 10'' jelly-roll pan. Bake until browned, about 15 minutes. Wrap bread rounds in foil. Warm in oven as meat cooks. Trim green onions, leaving about 1 inch of green tops. Cut onions lengthwise in strips. Remove bread rounds and meat from oven. Place each meat log on top of a bread round. Spoon Dilled Yogurt Sauce generously over meat. Sprinkle with onion strips. Garnish each sandwich with olives. Fold edge of bread over meat. Roll up to make a sandwich. Wrap 1 end of sandwich with a paper napkin. Makes 6 servings.

Scotch Broth

A hearty soup of lamb, barley and root vegetables, typical of the British Isles.

2 tablespoons vegetable oil
2 lbs. lamb shoulder, cut in 1/2-inch cubes,
   bones reserved
6 cups water
1 medium onion, sliced
1 leek, sliced
2 carrots, sliced

1 turnip, peeled, cut in 1/2-inch cubes
1 (16-oz.) can whole tomatoes
1 teaspoon salt
1 tablespoon chopped fresh parsley
1/2 cup pearl barley
1/4 teaspoon freshly ground black pepper

Heat 1 tablespoon oil in a large skillet. Add lamb cubes and bones; sauté until brown. Place lamb cubes and bones in a 6-quart pot. Add water. Bring to a boil. Skim foam from surface until surface is clear. Reduce heat. Cover and simmer 1 hour. Remove lamb and bones; discard bones. Pour liquid into a large bowl. Skim fat from surface until surface is clear. Wash pot. Heat remaining 1 tablespoon oil in clean pot. Add onion, leek, carrots and turnip. Sauté until onion is tender. Drain liquid from tomatoes. Add liquid to onion mixture. Dice tomatoes; add to onion mixture. Return lamb and cooking liquid to pot. Add salt, parsley, barley and pepper. Bring to a boil; reduce heat. Cover and simmer 45 minutes. Serve hot soup in heavy soup bowls or mugs. Makes 6 (2-cup) servings.

Open-Face Scandinavian Smørrebrød

These sandwiches are a work of art that are fun to do.

1/4 cup Dilled Yogurt Sauce, page 53
8 slices square thin-sliced pumpernickel
   bread or 8 slices square thin-sliced
   whole-wheat bread
2 tablespoons butter or margarine,
   room temperature
8 leaves Boston lettuce or
   other leaf lettuce
4 thin slices roast beef

1/4 cup Horseradish-Cream Sauce, page 49
4 sweet gherkins
1 (2-oz.) slice Danish Havarti cheese,
   cut in 8 triangles
4 radishes, thinly sliced
4 oz. smoked salmon or
   1 (4-3/8-oz.) can sardines, drained
4 hard-cooked eggs, each cut in 4 wedges
8 pitted black olives, sliced

Prepare Dilled Yogurt Sauce. Spread 1 side of each bread slice with butter or margarine. Place 2 slices side by side on each of 4 plates. Arrange lettuce leaves on each slice of bread. Roll up each slice of roast beef. Lay beef roll diagonally across 1 slice of bread on each plate. Spoon about 1 tablespoon Horseradish-Cream Sauce over each beef roll. Cut gherkins in 4 slices lengthwise, leaving slices attached at 1 end. Separate other end, forming fans. Place fans on 1 side of beef rolls. Arrange cheese triangles on other side of beef rolls. Surround cheese with radish slices. For the other sandwich, drizzle about 2 tablespoons Dilled Yogurt Sauce over each remaining slice of lettuce-covered bread. Fold salmon pieces in half. Arrange salmon pieces overlapping on each bread slice. If using sardines, lay 2 sardines on each slice. Arrange 4 egg wedges next to salmon pieces or sardines. Garnish with olive slices. Serve sandwiches immediately, with knives and forks. Makes 4 servings.

Caldo Gallego

Linguiça is a moderately spicy Portuguese sausage; pepperoni is a spicier substitute.

2 cups dried Great Northern beans
2 qts. water
1 chicken breast, skinned
1 meaty ham shank, cut in 3 pieces
2 beef bouillon cubes
2 chicken bouillon cubes
1/2 cup chopped onion

1/2 teaspoon salt
4 oz. linguiça sausage or pepperoni, sliced
2 medium potatoes, peeled,
   cut in 1/2-inch cubes
2 cups shredded cabbage, spinach or
   turnip greens

Sort and rinse beans; place in a 4-quart pot. Add water to a level 3 inches above beans. Bring beans and water to a boil. Boil 2 minutes. Remove from heat. Cover and let stand 1 hour. Drain beans, discarding water. Return beans to pot. Add 2 quarts water, chicken breast, ham-shank pieces, bouillon cubes, onion and salt. Bring mixture to a boil; reduce heat. Cover and simmer 30 minutes. Remove chicken breast and set aside. Continue cooking mixture until beans are tender, 1 to 1-1/2 hours. Remove ham shank. Set aside to cool. Add sausage, potatoes and cabbage, spinach or turnip greens. Simmer 20 minutes. Pull or cut ham and chicken from bones. Discard bones. Cut meat in 1/2-inch cubes. Add meat to pot. Simmer 10 minutes longer. Ladle hot soup into heavy bowls. Makes 6 (2-cup) servings.

How to Make Open-Face Scandinavian Smørrebrød

1/Lay beef roll across 1 slice of bread. Spoon Horseradish-Cream Sauce over beef. Arrange gherkins and cheese beside beef. Garnish with radishes.

2/For second sandwich, drizzle Dilled Yogurt Sauce over lettuce-covered bread. Fold salmon and arrange over lettuce. Garnish with olive slices and egg wedges.

Zucchini Avgolemono

A variation of the classic Greek lemon-rice soup.

6 cups Chicken Broth, page 16, or
  3 (14-1/2-oz.) cans regular-
  strength chicken broth
1/3 cup uncooked long-grain white rice
2 eggs

1/4 cup lemon juice
1 cup coarsely grated zucchini
Salt and freshly ground black pepper
  to taste
4 thin lemon slices

Bring broth to a boil in a large saucepan. Add rice; cover. Simmer over low heat 15 minutes. In a medium bowl, beat eggs until light colored and slightly thickened. Slowly beat in lemon juice. Remove 1 cup hot broth from saucepan. Slowly pour into egg mixture in a thin but steady stream, beating constantly. Set mixture aside. Stir grated zucchini into saucepan. Cover and simmer 5 minutes. Stir egg mixture into saucepan. Heat over low heat 3 to 5 minutes, stirring constantly. Do not boil or soup will curdle. Season to taste with salt and pepper. Ladle hot soup into individual bowls. Float a slice of lemon in each bowl. Makes 4 (1-1/2-cup) servings.

Minestrone   *Photo on cover.*

Cannellini beans or white kidney beans are common in Italian cooking.

1/4 cup olive oil
1 medium onion, sliced
2 garlic cloves, minced
2 carrots, sliced
2 celery stalks, sliced
1 leek, sliced
1 (28-oz.) can Italian plum tomatoes
1 qt. Chicken Broth, page 16, or
  2 (14-1/2-oz.) cans regular-
  strength chicken broth
1 tablespoon chopped fresh parsley

2 teaspoons dried leaf basil
1 teaspoon dried leaf oregano
1 teaspoon salt
1/4 teaspoon pepper
2 (15-oz.) cans cannellini beans or
  dark-red kidney beans, drained
2 cups shredded cabbage
1 medium zucchini, sliced
1/2 cup uncooked elbow or
  small-shell macaroni
Freshly grated Parmesan cheese

Heat olive oil in a 4-quart pot. Add onion, garlic, carrots, celery and leek. Sauté until onion is tender. Add tomatoes with liquid, breaking up tomatoes with a knife and fork. Stir in broth, parsley, basil, oregano, salt and pepper. Bring mixture to a boil; reduce heat. Cover and simmer 20 minutes. Stir in beans and cabbage. Simmer 10 minutes longer. Stir in zucchini and macaroni. Simmer, uncovered, 10 minutes. Serve with Parmesan cheese. Makes 6 (2-cup) servings.

Felafel

Garbanzo beans will mash easily if warmed first.

3 cups cooked garbanzo beans or
  2 (15-oz.) cans garbanzo beans,
  drained
3/4 cup fine fresh breadcrumbs
2 tablespoons sesame seeds
2 tablespoons chopped fresh parsley
2 tablespoons lemon juice
1 large garlic clove, minced
1/2 cup finely chopped onion
3/4 teaspoon salt
3/4 teaspoon ground cumin

1/4 teaspoon ground turmeric
1/8 teaspoon red (cayenne) pepper
1 egg, beaten
Whole-wheat flour
Oil for deep-frying
4 pita-bread rounds
Cucumber-Yogurt Sauce, page 52
2 cups shredded lettuce
1 cup alfalfa sprouts
2 fresh tomatoes, diced
3 green onions, sliced

Puree garbanzo beans in a blender, food processor or food mill. Or, mash beans with a potato masher. Place in a bowl. Stir in breadcrumbs, sesame seeds, parsley, lemon juice, garlic, onion, salt, cumin, turmeric and red pepper. Add egg. Form rounded tablespoons of bean mixture into balls. Roll balls in flour until lightly coated. Pour oil in a deep-fryer or large skillet until about 2 inches deep. Heat to 350F (175C) or until a 1-inch cube of bread added to the oil turns brown in 60 seconds. Fry balls, 4 or 5 at a time, until golden brown, about 3 minutes. Drain on paper towels. Keep warm in a 300F (150C) oven. Cut bread rounds in half. Spoon about 1 tablespoon Cucumber-Yogurt Sauce into each half. Place 3 balls in each half. Arrange pocket halves on a platter with lettuce, sprouts, tomatoes and green onions. Individuals add vegetables and sauce to Felafel, as desired. Makes 4 servings.

Mulligatawny

Indian curry-flavored soup has a slight "bite" which explains its name—meaning "pepper water."

2 tablespoons vegetable oil
2 lbs. meaty chicken pieces
2 tablespoons butter or margarine
1 cup chopped onion
2 carrots, sliced
1/2 cup chopped green bell pepper
1 large tart green apple, peeled, diced
2 tablespoons all-purpose flour
2 teaspoons curry powder
2 teaspoons salt
1/2 teaspoon ground mace

1 qt. Chicken Broth, page 16, or
   2 (14-1/2-oz.) cans regular-
   strength chicken broth
3 cups water
1/2 cup tomato sauce
1 bay leaf
2 whole cloves
1/2 teaspoon coarsely ground black pepper
Pinch red (cayenne) pepper
1 cup apple juice
Rice with Raisins, see below

Rice with Raisins:
1-1/2 cups water
1/2 teaspoon salt
1/4 teaspoon ground mace

1/2 cup golden raisins
3/4 cup uncooked long-grain white rice
1/4 cup slivered almonds

Heat oil in a large skillet. Add chicken pieces; brown lightly. Remove chicken. Melt butter or margarine in a 6-quart pot. Add onion, carrots, green pepper and apple. Sauté until onion is tender. In a small bowl, combine flour, curry powder, salt and mace. Sprinkle flour mixture over onion mixture; stir to combine. Gradually add broth, water and tomato sauce to pot, stirring constantly. Add browned chicken pieces, bay leaf, cloves, black pepper and red pepper to pot. Bring mixture to a boil, stirring constantly. Reduce heat. Cover and simmer 1 hour. Remove chicken pieces. Strain cooking liquid through a fine sieve. Discard bay leaf and cloves. Force vegetables through sieve with the back of a spoon. Return liquid to pot. Spoon fat from surface. Pull strips of paper towel across surface of liquid to remove any fat. Remove skin from chicken. Pull meat from bones. Discard skin and bones. Cut meat in 1/2-inch cubes. Stir chicken meat and apple juice into pot. Simmer 10 to 15 minutes. Prepare Rice with Raisins. To serve, spoon about 1/3 cup Rice with Raisins into each bowl. Ladle hot soup over rice. Makes 6 (2-cup) servings.

Rice with Raisins:
Bring water to a boil in a small saucepan. Add salt and mace. Slowly sprinkle raisins and rice into water, maintaining a boil. Reduce heat to lowest setting. Cover and simmer 20 minutes or until water has been absorbed and rice is tender. Add almonds to rice; toss. Keep warm until ready to serve.

Freeze soups in jars or containers with straight sides so soup can be removed easily before it is fully thawed.

Russian Chlodnik

Serve icy cold in glass punch cups or bowls to show off the pretty pink color.

1 (6-3/4-oz.) can small shrimp, drained
1 tablespoon butter or margarine
2 tablespoons chopped green onion
1 teaspoon dried dillweed
1 tablespoon lemon juice
3 cups buttermilk

1 (16-oz.) can small whole beets, drained
1/2 medium cucumber, peeled, shredded
1/2 teaspoon salt
1/8 teaspoon white pepper
2 sliced hard-cooked eggs, if desired
6 sprigs parsley or fresh dillweed

Rinse shrimp under running cold water. Melt butter or margarine in a 3-quart saucepan. Add shrimp and green onion; sauté 30 seconds. Remove from heat. Sprinkle dried dillweed and lemon juice over shrimp mixture; toss lightly. Stir buttermilk into shrimp mixture. Thinly slice beets of 1-inch diameter or less. Cut larger beets in half; slice. Add sliced beets, cucumber, salt and white pepper to shrimp mixture. Pour soup into an airtight container. Refrigerate at least 4 hours. Serve in small soup bowls or a glass serving bowl. Garnish with fresh parsley or dillweed. Or, if desired, float slices of hard-cooked egg on soup with a sprig of parsley or dillweed on top. Makes 6 (3/4-cup) servings.

French Onion Soup au Gratin

Slowly cooking the onions to a deep-golden color creates a full rich flavor.

1/3 cup butter or margarine
2 tablespoons vegetable oil
1 garlic clove, minced
2 lbs. yellow onions, sliced
1/2 teaspoon sugar
1/4 teaspoon dried leaf thyme
1/4 teaspoon white pepper
1/4 cup dry red wine
3 (10-1/2-oz.) cans concentrated beef broth
1 (14-1/2-oz.) can regular-strength
   chicken broth

1 teaspoon Worcestershire sauce
3 tablespoons butter or margarine,
   room temperature
1/4 teaspoon paprika
6 tablespoons freshly grated Parmesan cheese
   (1-1/4 oz.)
6 slices French bread
1-1/2 cups shredded Gruyère or Swiss cheese
   (6 oz.)

Combine 1/3 cup butter or margarine and oil in a 4-quart pot. Heat until butter or margarine melts. Add garlic, onion and sugar. Sauté over medium-low heat until onions are golden, about 20 minutes. Do not allow onions to brown. Sprinkle thyme and white pepper over onions. Stir in red wine, beef and chicken broth, and Worcestershire sauce. Bring to a boil; reduce heat. Cover and simmer 15 minutes. Preheat broiler. In a small bowl, combine 3 tablespoons butter or margarine, paprika and Parmesan cheese. Cream with the back of a spoon until smooth. Toast 1 side of each bread slice under broiler. Turn slices over. Spread untoasted side with butter mixture. Broil until browned and bubbly. Ladle soup into 6 individual casseroles or ovenproof soup bowls. Float 1 piece toast on each serving. Sprinkle 1/4 cup shredded Gruyère or Swiss cheese over top. Place casseroles or bowls under broiler until cheese melts. Serve each casserole or bowl on a plate. Makes 6 (1-1/2-cup) servings.

Party Ideas

ood brings people together. A gathering of friends is more enjoyable when good food is added. With the more relaxed styles of entertaining today, guests like to participate. Making their own sandwich or cooking their own soup creates a casual, festive atmosphere. Soups and sandwiches are fun party foods for everyone.

Serve Chinese Hot Pot for a small dinner party. Set the bubbling soup in the middle of the table. Guests cook their own steak, seafood and vegetables in the hot soup. Small bowls of spicy sauces are set at each place for dunking the just-cooked morsels. For an authentic Chinese meal, use chopsticks to hold the food as it cooks. Fondue forks don't fit this theme, but make cooking-your-own easier. End the meal by ladling broth, enriched by the flavor of meat and vegetables, into bowls.

For large parties, serve Posole buffet-style. Guests help themselves to bowls of Posole, a flavorful Mexican pork, bean and corn soup. Topping of avocado, green onion, cilantro, cheese, radish, lettuce and sour cream can be sprinkled or spooned over the top.

Soups and sandwiches fit both casual and formal entertaining. Brandied Scallops in Melon Boats or Artist's Palette would be elegant fare for an anniversary brunch or bridal shower. For a casual party, try a hearty homemade soup and biscuits. Louisiana Creole Gumbo is a thick, tasty soup teaming with seafood and chicken in a rich tomato broth. It's good Cajun cooking that may be new to some and will be enjoyed by all.

When it's your turn for a party, bring friends together around a steaming bowl of soup or a mouth-watering sandwich. Either could be the focus or a fancy addition to a party meal. ✿❀

Menu

Cajun Gumbo Supper

Louisiana Creole Gumbo, page 144
Buttermilk Biscuits
Fresh Spinach, Orange
& Red-Onion Salad
French Dressing
Kahlúa-Coffee Slices, page 148

Family Backyard Picnic

Barbecue Hot-Dog Ring, page 138
Goliath Burger, page 141
Baked Beans
Potato Chips
Marshmallow-Iced Brownies, page 156
Soft Drinks

Posole

Serve buffet-style in an earthenware tureen surrounded by toppers.

1 cup dried pinto beans, sorted
2 tablespoons vegetable oil
2 lbs. boneless pork, cut in 1-inch cubes
8 chicken drumsticks or thighs
1 cup chopped onion
2 garlic cloves, minced
2 qts. water
2 teaspoons salt
1 teaspoon dried leaf oregano
1/2 teaspoon ground cumin
1/4 teaspoon pepper

1 (28-oz.) can whole tomatoes, diced
1 tablespoon chili powder
2 (15-oz.) cans golden hominy, drained
Posole Toppers:
  1 avocado, sliced
  1/2 cup sliced green onions
  1/2 cup chopped cilantro
  1 cup dairy sour cream
  1 cup shredded Monterey Jack cheese
  1/2 cup sliced radishes
  2 cups shredded lettuce

Rinse beans. Place beans in a saucepan with water to cover by 2 inches. Boil; boil 2 minutes. Remove from heat. Cover and let stand 1 hour. Drain beans. Heat 1 tablespoon oil in a skillet. Brown half the pork cubes. Lift pork cubes from skillet; set aside. Repeat with remaining pork cubes. Brown chicken pieces in remaining hot oil; set aside. Wipe skillet clean. Heat remaining oil in skillet. Add onion and garlic. Sauté until onion is tender. In a large pot, combine beans, pork cubes, onion mixture, 2 quarts water, salt, oregano, cumin and pepper. Bring to a boil; reduce heat. Cover and simmer 45 minutes. Add tomatoes and juice, chicken, chili powder and hominy to pot. Simmer 30 minutes. Ladle soup into bowls, including 1 drumstick or thigh in each serving. Guests sprinkle Posole Toppers over their serving. Makes 8 (2-cup) servings.

Cioppino

A traditional San Francisco seafood soup, served with sourdough bread.

2 tablespoons olive oil
1-1/2 cups chopped onion
3 garlic cloves, minced
1 (16-oz.) can whole tomatoes, diced
1 cup dry white wine
2 cups tomato juice
1 qt. Fish Broth (4 cups), page 20
1 bay leaf
1/4 teaspoon dried leaf basil

1/4 teaspoon dried leaf thyme
1/2 teaspoon salt
1 cooked Dungeness crab or
  4 small uncooked lobster tails
24 mussels or clams
2 lbs. sea bass, halibut or cod,
  cut in 8 pieces
1 lb. medium, deveined, shelled raw shrimp
1/2 cup chopped fresh parsley

Heat oil in a large pot. Add onion and garlic. Sauté until tender. Add tomatoes and juice, wine, tomato juice and broth to onion. In a cheesecloth bag, tie together bay leaf, basil and thyme; add bag and salt to pot. Simmer 10 minutes. Crack top shell of crab. Lift off shell; discard. Remove and discard internal organs. Pull off under-plate; discard. Break crab into separate legs, including meaty knuckles. If using lobster tails, cut each into 2 pieces. Rinse mussels or clams in cool water. Gently scrub shells. Add crab or lobster and mussels or clams to pot. Bring to a boil; reduce heat. Cover and simmer 10 minutes. Add fish and shrimp. Simmer until mussel shells open and shrimp turn pink, about 10 minutes. Discard herb bag and any mussels or clams that remain closed. Arrange 1 crab leg or piece of lobster, 3 mussels or clams, 6 shrimp and 1 piece of fish in each of 8 shallow bowls. Ladle hot broth over seafood. Garnish with parsley. Makes 8 servings.

Flower Buffet Sandwich

Bake your favorite bread in a 9-inch pie plate to form a round loaf for this party treat.

Dilled Salmon Spread, see below
Cucumber & Cheese Spread, see below
Egg Salad, see below
1 (1-lb.) round loaf sourdough white bread
1 medium avocado
1 tablespoon lime or lemon juice
1/4 teaspoon salt
2 tablespoons mayonnaise

1 green onion, sliced
1 (8-oz.) pkg. cream cheese,
** room temperature**
3 tablespoons dairy sour cream
1 cup alfalfa sprouts
1 medium tomato
Curly endive
Cherry tomatoes for garnish

Dilled Salmon Spread:
1 (6-3/4-oz.) can salmon, drained
1 (3-oz.) pkg. cream cheese,
** room temperature**

1/4 cup dairy sour cream
3/4 teaspoon dried dillweed
Onion powder to taste

Cucumber & Cheese Spread:
1 (3-oz.) pkg. cream cheese,
** room temperature**
1 tablespoon dairy sour cream

2 tablespoons mayonnaise
1/2 medium cucumber, peeled
2 oz. blue cheese, crumbled

Egg Salad:
2 hard-cooked eggs
2 tablespoons mayonnaise
1 tablespoon dairy sour cream

1 teaspoon prepared mustard
Salt to taste
Red (cayenne) pepper to taste

Prepare spreads and Egg Salad. Refrigerate at least 2 hours or overnight. Cut bread in 4 slices horizontally. Cut top slice into a daisy with 5 petals. Set daisy shape aside. Using a round 8-inch pan as a guide, cut crusts from remaining slices. Peel avocado; slice flesh. Place in a blender or food processor. Add lime or lemon juice, salt, mayonnaise and green onion; process until smooth. In a small bowl, beat cream cheese and sour cream until smooth. Place bottom slice of bread on a serving platter. Spread with Dilled Salmon Spread. Top with another slice of bread. Spread with Cucumber & Cheese Spread. Top with remaining bread slice. Spread sides of sandwich with cheese mixture. Spread avocado mixture on top of sandwich stack. Sprinkle alfalfa sprouts over avocado mixture. Cut sandwich stack top to bottom into 10 wedges. Spread daisy top and sides with Egg Salad. Place on top of sandwich, Egg-Salad-side up. Cut peel from tomato in 1 continuous spiral. Starting at 1 end, coil tomato peel, shiny-side out, forming a rose. Place tomato rose in center of daisy petals. Surround base of sandwich with endive and tomatoes. Refrigerate sandwich until ready to serve, up to 2 hours. Makes 10 servings.

Dilled Salmon Spread:
Remove small bones and skin from salmon. Flake salmon with a fork. In a small bowl, beat cream cheese and sour cream with an electric mixer until smooth. Stir in dillweed and onion powder to taste. Add flaked salmon. Refrigerate until ready to use.

Cucumber & Cheese Spread:
Combine cream cheese, sour cream and mayonnaise in a small bowl. Beat with an electric mixer until smooth. Coarsely shred cucumber. Stir cucumber and crumbled blue cheese into cheese mixture. Refrigerate until ready to use.

Egg Salad:
Press hard-cooked eggs through a sieve into a small bowl. Stir in mayonnaise, sour cream, mustard, salt and red pepper. Refrigerate until ready to use.

How to Make Flower Buffet Sandwich

1/Cut bread in 4 crosswise slices. Cut top slice into a daisy with 5 petals.

2/Place tomato rose in center of daisy. Surround base of sandwich with endive and cherry tomatoes.

Shrimp Newberg en Croissant

For an elegant luncheon, serve with fresh fruit topped with a combination of yogurt and whipped cream.

3 tablespoons butter or margarine
2 garlic cloves
1 lb. medium, deveined, peeled raw shrimp
2 tablespoons all-purpose flour
1/2 teaspoon paprika
1/4 teaspoon salt
1-1/2 cups half and half

1 egg yolk, beaten
1/2 cup dry white wine
1 tablespoon dry sherry
White pepper to taste
6 Croissants, page 44, or other croissants
Fresh watercress

Melt butter or margarine in a medium skillet. Crush garlic with flat side of a knife, keeping garlic in 1 piece. Add garlic and shrimp to skillet. Sauté over medium heat until shrimp turn bright pink. Remove shrimp; set aside. Remove and discard garlic. Add flour, paprika and salt to pan drippings; stir until smooth. Remove from heat. Gradually stir in half and half. Bring to a boil, stirring constantly. Stir a small amount of hot mixture into egg yolk. Return egg mixture to skillet. Cook 1 minute longer. Add wine, sherry, shrimp and white pepper to taste. Cook over low heat, stirring occasionally. Do not boil. Cut almost through each croissant horizontally. Open carefully without splitting in half. Place 1 croissant on each plate. Spoon shrimp mixture in open croissant. Close croissant. Garnish with a sprig of watercress. Serve immediately. Makes 6 servings.

Linguiça-Rice Torta

This torta is a sausage-and-vegetable-filled bread baked in a tart pan.

1 tomato, peeled, cored
2 tablespoons vegetable oil
1-1/2 cups uncooked long-grain white rice
1 garlic clove, minced
1 cup chopped onion
1/2 cup chopped green bell pepper
1 teaspoon ground cumin
1 teaspoon salt
2 cups hot Chicken Broth, page 16, or
   1 (14-1/2-oz.) can regular-
   strength chicken broth

8 oz. linguiça sausage, sliced, or
   other fully cooked sausage
1 cup frozen baby green peas
1 (2-oz.) jar pimiento-stuffed olives,
   drained
1 (8-oz.) can refrigerated crescent rolls
2 eggs
1 tablespoon milk

Cut tomato in half horizontally. Using a spoon or your thumb, remove and discard seeds; dice tomato. In a large skillet with tight-fitting lid, heat oil over medium-high heat; add rice. Stir until rice turns light brown. Add garlic, onion and green pepper; stir until onion is tender. Sprinkle diced tomato, cumin and salt over rice; stir in. Pour hot broth into skillet; bring to a boil. Reduce heat to lowest setting. Cover and simmer 15 minutes. Stir in sausage, peas and olives. Remove from heat. Preheat oven to 375F (190C). Grease a 10-inch tart pan or 8-inch springform pan. Separate crescent-roll dough into 4 rectangles. On a lightly floured board, put 2 rectangles side by side with long sides touching. Pinch rectangles together. Press diagonal perforations to seal each rectangle. Roll out dough to a 13-inch square. Using a pan lid as a guide, cut out a 13-inch circle. Place dough in greased pan. Roll out remaining dough and cut a circle 1 inch larger than tart pan or springform pan used. Reserve dough trimmings. Separate 1 egg; reserve egg yolk in a small bowl. Add remaining egg to egg white; beat until blended. Stir egg into rice mixture. Spoon rice mixture into lined pan. Place remaining dough circle on top of filling. Fold edges under and tuck into sides of pan. Beat together reserved egg yolk and milk. Brush on top of torta. Cut dough trimmings in long thin strips. Weave strips in a crisscross pattern on top of torta. Brush with yolk mixture. Bake until golden brown, about 25 minutes. Cool in pan 10 minutes. Carefully remove from pan. Cut in wedges. Serve warm. Makes 8 servings.

Barbecue Hot-Dog Ring

A wheel of hot dogs that is pulled apart for guests to help themselves.

3 tablespoons bottled barbecue sauce
3/4 cup buttermilk
3 cups biscuit mix
4 (1-oz.) slices American cheese

8 hot dogs or precooked sausages
Tangy-Sweet Spread, page 46, or
   hot-dog relish

Preheat oven to 375F (190C). In a small bowl, stir together barbecue sauce and buttermilk. Measure biscuit mix into a large bowl. Pour buttermilk mixture over biscuit mix; stir lightly just until biscuit mix is moistened. Turn out dough onto a lightly floured board. Knead with your finger tips 10 times. Roll out dough to a 10-inch circle. Cut into 8 equal wedges. Cut cheese slices in half diagonally. Place 1 cheese triangle and 1 hot dog or sausage on the wide end of each wedge of dough. Starting at wide end, roll up hot dog and cheese in dough. Arrange hot dogs, pointing inward like the spokes of a wheel, on an ungreased baking sheet with the point of the dough wedge facing down. Sides of hot dogs should almost touch. Leave center of wheel open. Bake until browned, about 20 minutes. Slide hot-dog ring onto a serving platter. Place a bowl of Tangy-Sweet Spread or hot-dog relish in center of ring. Makes 8 servings.

How to Make Barbecue Hot-Dog Ring

1/Cut dough into 8 equal wedges. Cut cheese slices in half diagonally. Place 1 cheese triangle and 1 hot dog or sausage on the wide end of each wedge of dough.

2/Roll up meat and cheese in dough. Arrange rolls, meat pointing inward like the spokes of a wheel, on ungreased baking sheet with point of dough wedge facing down.

Savory Roast-Beef Loaf

Beef rubbed with spices, roasted and wrapped in an herb-flavored bread.

Cucumber-Yogurt Sauce, page 52
1 (3-1/2- to 4-lb.) beef eye-of-
   round roast or beef rib-eye roast
2 tablespoons olive oil
1 tablespoon red-wine vinegar
1/4 cup chopped fresh parsley
1 garlic clove, minced
1 teaspoon salt

1 teaspoon ground fenugreek
1 teaspoon dried mint
1/2 teaspoon ground cumin
Cottage-Cheese Dough, see below
1 bunch fresh spinach, washed,
   stems removed
1 egg
2 tablespoons milk

Cottage-Cheese Dough:
1/4 cup warm water (105F, 40C)
1 (1/4-oz.) pkg. active dry yeast
   (1 tablespoon)
1 teaspoon sugar
1 cup creamed cottage cheese (8 oz.)
1/2 cup warm milk (105F, 40C)

1 egg, beaten
1 teaspoon dried dillweed
1 teaspoon dried onion flakes
1/2 teaspoon salt
3-1/2 to 4 cups all-purpose flour

Prepare Cucumber-Yogurt Sauce. Refrigerate until ready to serve. Place beef roast in a baking pan. In a small bowl, combine olive oil, vinegar, parsley, garlic, salt, fenugreek, mint and cumin. Rub seasoning mixture over roast. Cover loosely with a towel or waxed paper. Refrigerate at least 2 hours or up to 24 hours. Prepare Cottage-Cheese Dough. While dough rises, roast beef as follows: Preheat oven to 350F (175C). Place roast on a rack in a shallow pan. Insert meat thermometer into center of roast. Roast until thermometer registers 120F (50C), about 40 minutes. Remove from oven; cool. Preheat oven to 375F (190C). Grease baking sheet. Punch down dough by pushing your fist into center; pull edges of dough over center. Turn out dough on a lightly floured board. Knead 5 times. Roll out dough into a rectangle about 2 inches longer and 8 inches wider than roast. Arrange a layer of spinach leaves on dough. Place roast on spinach leaves. Cover roast with remaining spinach leaves. Pull up long sides of dough, fitting dough tightly around roast. Trim off any excess dough. Pinch seams to seal. Pull up dough at ends tightly; trim excess. Pinch to seal. Place loaf on greased baking sheet, seam-side down. Form dough trimmings into long thin ropes. Crisscross ropes over top of loaf. In a small bowl, beat egg and milk; brush over loaf. Bake until richly browned, 25 to 30 minutes. Let stand 5 to 10 minutes before slicing. Slice to serve. Serve warm or cold with Cucumber-Yogurt Sauce. Makes 8 servings.

Cottage-Cheese Dough:
In a large bowl, combine 1/4 cup warm water, yeast and sugar. Stir to dissolve. Set aside until foamy, about 15 minutes. Add cottage cheese, warm milk, egg, dillweed, onion flakes, salt and 1-1/2 cups flour. Beat until smooth. Add remaining flour, 1/2 cup at a time, until dough pulls away from sides of bowl. On a lightly floured surface, knead dough until smooth and elastic, 5 to 10 minutes. Clean and grease bowl. Place dough in bowl, turning to grease all sides. Cover bowl with a dry towel. Let rise in a warm place until doubled in size, about 2 hours.

Artist's Palette

Sandwiches en gelée are the canvas for a vegetable design.

12 slices Squaw Bread, page 42, or
  other dark rye bread
2 (5-oz.) pkgs. cream cheese with
  garlic and herbs, room temperature
12 (1-oz.) slices sandwich ham
1 (.25-oz.) envelope unflavored gelatin
2 tablespoons dry white wine
1 cup Chicken Broth, page 16, or
  canned regular-strength chicken broth

2/3 cup mayonnaise
1/3 cup dairy sour cream
Salt and white pepper to taste
Garnishes: cooked fresh or canned
  asparagus tips, green onions, pitted
  black olives, cherry tomatoes,
  green peas, pimiento strips,
  dill sprigs and green grapes

Spread bread generously with cheese. Cut ham slices the size and shape of bread. Save trimmings for another use. Lay ham slices on cheese. Place sandwiches on a platter. Cover with a damp cloth. Refrigerate until needed. In a small bowl, combine gelatin and wine; let stand 5 minutes to soften. Bring broth to a boil in small saucepan. Pour gelatin mixture into hot broth; stir until dissolved. Cool gelatin mixture 15 minutes. Stir in mayonnaise and sour cream. Season to taste with salt and white pepper. Arrange chilled sandwiches on a cooling rack, spacing them 2 inches apart. Pour half the mayonnaise mixture into a small bowl. Place ice and cold water 2 inches deep in a large bowl. Place saucepan with remaining mayonnaise mixture in ice water. Stir until mixture becomes syrupy. Spoon syrupy mayonnaise mixture slowly over each sandwich. Refrigerate sandwiches until set, 10 to 15 minutes. Pour reserved mayonnaise mixture into saucepan. Melt over low heat if necessary, stirring constantly. Set saucepan in ice water; stir until syrupy. Spoon over sandwiches again. Repeat process with any remaining mayonnaise mixture. Refrigerate sandwiches until ready to serve. For garnish, arrange asparagus tips or green-onion pieces in a spread-fan shape on top of each sandwich. Complete the garnish with ripe-olive pieces, cherry tomatoes, green peas, pimiento and dill sprigs. Serve sandwiches on lettuce-lined plates garnished with grapes. Makes 12 servings.

How to Make Artist's Palette

1/Arrange chilled sandwiches 2 inches apart on a rack. Spoon syrupy mayonnaise mixture slowly over sandwiches.

2/Garnish each sandwich as desired. Serve individual sandwiches on lettuce leaves garnished with grapes.

Goliath Burger

Cook this giant burger outside on a charcoal grill or in the oven.

1 Goliath Sesame-Seed Bun, page 55	**1/3 cup Special Hamburger Sauce, page 33**
1-1/2 lbs. ground beef	**4 large leaves salad-bowl lettuce or**
1 cup fine fresh breadcrumbs	**red-leaf lettuce**
1-1/2 teaspoons salt	**1 large red onion, sliced**
1/4 teaspoon pepper	**2 tomatoes, sliced**
1/4 cup concentrated beef broth	**1 cup dill-pickle slices**
1 teaspoon Worcestershire sauce	**Ketchup**
6 oz. American cheese, sliced	**Mustard**

Prepare Goliath Sesame-Seed Bun. Preheat oven to 350F (175C). In a large bowl, combine ground beef, breadcrumbs, salt, pepper, broth and Worcestershire sauce. Shape meat mixture into a large patty, 10 inches in diameter; place on a 15" x 10" jelly-roll pan. Bake, without turning, until well browned, about 40 minutes. Arrange cheese slices over top. Bake until cheese melts, about 5 minutes longer. Split bun crosswise. Spread Special Hamburger Sauce over bottom part of bun. Arrange lettuce on bun so curly edges slightly overhang bun edge. Carefully place meat patty on top of lettuce. Arrange onion, tomatoes and pickles on patty. Place top part of bun on patty, cut-side down. To serve, cut in wedges. Pass ketchup and mustard. Makes 6 servings.

Brandied Scallops in Melon Boats

Serve with warm Croissants, page 44, for a summer brunch.

5 tablespoons butter or margarine
2 tablespoons minced shallots
1 tablespoon lemon juice
12 oz. fresh or thawed frozen scallops
2 tablespoons brandy
3 tablespoons all-purpose flour
2 cups Chicken Broth, page 16, or
   1 (14-1/2-oz.) can regular-
   strength chicken broth

1 egg
1-1/2 cups half and half
1/4 cup dry white wine
1/2 teaspoon salt
1/4 teaspoon white pepper
3 medium cantaloupe
1 tablespoon minced chives

Melt 2 tablespoons butter or margarine in a medium skillet. Add shallots; sauté 1 minute. Add lemon juice and scallops. Sauté until scallops are just firm and opaque, 3 to 5 minutes. In a small metal cup or pan, heat brandy until warm, about 150F (65C). Pour over scallops; carefully ignite. Allow flames to burn out; set aside. In a medium saucepan, melt remaining 3 tablespoons butter or margarine. Stir in flour until smooth. Gradually add broth, stirring constantly. Stir over medium heat until mixture boils. Reduce heat to low. Beat egg in a small bowl. Add half and half and wine; beat until well mixed. Pour egg mixture in a thin stream into hot broth while stirring. Add salt, pepper and scallop mixture. Simmer over low heat 5 minutes, stirring occasionally. Do not boil. Remove from heat. Pour into a storage container or casserole with a lid. Refrigerate until well chilled, at least 4 hours. Cut each cantaloupe in half lengthwise. Using a spoon, scoop out seeds and discard. Scoop out flesh from cantaloupes leaving 1-inch shells. Use cantaloupe flesh for another purpose. Place cantaloupe halves on individual plates. Ladle chilled soup into each cantaloupe bowl. Sprinkle chives over each serving. Makes 6 servings.

Substituting Commercially Canned Broth for Homemade

Commercially canned broths come in regular-strength and concentrated or double-strength. Concentrated beef and chicken broth comes in 10-1/2-ounce or 10-3/4-ounce cans. These cans hold about 1-1/4 cups of broth. To substitute these broths for homemade, dilute them with an equal volume of water.

   Regular-strength beef and chicken broth come in cans of various sizes. Substitute these broths for an equal volume of homemade broth.

Chinese Hot Pot

A Chinese fondue dinner where the cooking liquid becomes the soup.

2 lbs. beef flank steak, beef
   top-round steak or beef sirloin steak
2 qts. Chicken Broth, page 16, or
   4-1/2 (14-1/2-oz.) cans regular-
   strength chicken broth
1 garlic clove, minced
1 tablespoon sliced peeled gingerroot
2 green onions, sliced
1/4 cup soy sauce
1 tablespoon dry sherry

2 cups packed fresh spinach leaves
3 oz. cellophane noodles or
   2 cups cooked long-grain white rice
1 lb. tofu (bean curd), cubed
1 bok choy or Chinese cabbage
12 large fresh mushrooms, sliced
1 (5-oz.) can bamboo shoots, drained
1/2 lb. Chinese pea pods
Mustard Dipping Sauce, see below
Soy-Sesame Dipping Sauce, see below

Mustard Dipping Sauce:
1/3 cup chicken broth
3 tablespoons soy sauce
4 teaspoons dry mustard

2 teaspoons cornstarch
2 tablespoons cold water

Soy-Sesame Dipping Sauce:
1/4 cup soy sauce
1 tablespoon honey
1 tablespoon brown sugar
1/2 cup water
1 teaspoon dry sherry

1/2 teaspoon sesame oil
1 tablespoon cornstarch
2 tablespoons cold water
2 tablespoons toasted sesame seeds

Place beef in freezer until firm but not frozen, about 1 hour. In a 4-quart pot, combine broth, garlic, gingerroot and green onions. Cover and simmer 30 minutes. Slice beef as thinly as possible across the grain. Place in a medium bowl. Combine soy sauce and sherry; pour over beef strips. Stir until beef is well-coated; set aside. Rinse spinach; trim and shred. Soak cellophane noodles in 2 cups hot water 30 minutes; drain. Arrange noodles or rice and spinach on a platter. Arrange tofu cubes on another platter. Rinse and trim wilted leaves and root end of bok choy or Chinese cabbage; cut in bite-size pieces. Arrange bok choy or cabbage pieces, mushroom slices, bamboo shoots and pea pods on platter with tofu. Keep each vegetable separate. Leave space for marinated beef strips; set platter aside. Prepare dipping sauces. Set at each place setting. Preheat Mongolian fire pot or set up fondue pot or electric skillet on table. Pour hot broth into pot or skillet. Bring to a boil. Remove beef strips from marinade; discard marinade. Place beef on platter with tofu and vegetables; pass platter. Guests use chopsticks or fondue forks to cook their own beef and vegetables in simmering broth; then dip in sauces. When beef and vegetables are cooked, add shredded spinach and cellophane noodles or cooked rice to broth. Simmer 2 to 3 minutes. Ladle hot broth into individual bowls. Makes 6 servings.

Mustard Dipping Sauce:
Bring broth and soy sauce to a boil in a small saucepan. In a small bowl, combine mustard and cornstarch. Add cold water, stirring until smooth. Pour mustard mixture into broth mixture, stirring constantly. Bring sauce to a boil, stirring constantly. Pour sauce into 6 small individual bowls.

Soy-Sesame Dipping Sauce:
In a small saucepan, combine soy sauce, honey, brown sugar, water, sherry and sesame oil. Bring to a boil. In a small bowl, combine cornstarch and cold water, stirring until smooth. Gradually pour cornstarch mixture into soy mixture, stirring constantly. Bring sauce to a boil, stirring constantly. Add toasted sesame seeds. Pour sauce into 6 small individual bowls.

Louisiana Creole Gumbo

Serve as part of a Cajun dinner with hot biscuits and pecan pie.

3 lbs. chicken pieces
2 cups water
1-1/2 cups chopped onion
1/2 cup chopped celery leaves or
    chopped celery
1 small carrot, sliced
1/2 teaspoon salt
1 bay leaf
6 tablespoons vegetable oil
6 tablespoons all-purpose flour
2 tablespoons butter or margarine
1 medium, green bell pepper, diced
1 (28-oz.) can whole tomatoes

2 cups Chicken Broth, page 16, or
    1 (14-1/2-oz.) can regular-
    strength chicken broth
2 bay leaves
1/2 teaspoon dried leaf thyme
1 dried red pepper, if desired
24 medium, raw shrimp (about 8 oz.)
16 scallops
1 lb. fresh okra, sliced, or
    2 (9-oz.) pkgs. frozen cut okra
2 teaspoons gumbo filé powder
3 cups cooked rice
Hot-pepper sauce

In a 4-quart pot, combine chicken, water, 1 cup chopped onion, celery leaves or celery, carrot, salt and bay leaf. Bring to a boil; reduce heat. Cover and simmer until chicken is tender, about 40 minutes. Remove chicken pieces; cool. Remove skin from chicken. Pull meat from bones; discard skin and bones. Dice chicken meat; set aside. Strain cooking liquid, discarding vegetables. Spoon fat from surface of liquid. Pull strips of paper towels across surface of liquid to remove any fat. In a heavy skillet, heat oil. Add flour; stir over medium-low heat until mixture turns dark brown. Set aside. In a 4- or 6-quart pot, melt butter or margarine. Add remaining 1/2 cup onion and green pepper. Sauté until onion is tender. Drain juice from tomatoes into pot. Dice tomatoes; stir into onion mixture. Add reserved flour mixture, cooking liquid from chicken, broth, 2 bay leaves, thyme and red pepper, if desired. Stir to combine. Simmer 15 minutes. Shell and devein shrimp; add shrimp, scallops, okra and reserved chicken meat to pot. Simmer 15 minutes longer. Remove and discard bay leaves and red pepper. Ladle 1 cup soup into a small bowl. Stir in gumbo filé powder until smooth; return to pot. Stir until soup thickens slightly. Do not boil. Ladle hot gumbo into individual bowls. Top each with about 1/3 cup cooked rice. Pass hot-pepper sauce to sprinkle on top. Makes 8 (2-cup) servings.

Desserts

Soups or sandwiches for dessert sound unusual, but actually they are very common and popular ends to a meal. Fruit soups or fruit-and-wine soups are lightly sweet and refreshing. They are not as rich as many desserts. Scandinavian Fruit Soup, probably the best-known dessert soup, is enjoyed around the world with many variations. Cookies sandwiched with flavored icings or ice cream are family favorites. They top the list of popular dessert sandwiches. They also make great snacks because they are easy to eat.

Dessert soups offer a variety of experiences. They can be served hot, cold, gelled or frozen. Cherry-Dumpling Soup has doughnut-hole dumplings floating in steaming hot cherry soup. Jellied Strawberry-Swirl Soup softly mounds on a spoon, then melts in your mouth. Frozen Strawberry-Banana Soup is an island of frozen fruit surrounded by sparkling strawberry soda.

Most dessert soups are made from fruit, but some are pudding-like. Chilled Pumpkin Bisque tastes like a spicy pumpkin pie served in a bowl.

Dessert sandwiches are fun to create because the possibilities are almost endless. The sandwich base could be cake, cookies, pastry or even bread. Sandwich fillings can be icing, ice cream, custard, fruit or cream. Strawberry Ribbons are layers of nutty pastry enclosing a luscious strawberry-cream filling. Fresh strawberries top the glazed pastry layer. Maple-nut ice cream is the filling for Ginger-Nut Waffle Sandwich. Ice cream is sandwiched between unusual gingerbread waffles. Paradise Wedges start with plain white bread. A filling of cream cheese and pineapple and a crunchy coating of peanuts and coconut transform a simple sandwich into a delicate dessert.

Dessert soups and sandwiches will fit any occasion and meet any need. A simple fruit-and-wine soup will add a final light, sweet touch to a filling meal. Or, serve extra-special Cherry-Chocolate Alaska Layers when dessert will be the high point. You will find a suitable occasion to enjoy them all. 🌺

Menu

Baby-Shower Buffet

Pastel Mints & Mixed Nuts
Jellied Strawberry-Swirl Soup, page 151
Paradise Wedges, page 153
Lemonade Punch

Bon-Voyage Dessert

Oregon Blackberry Soup, page 147
Ginger-Nut Waffle Sandwich, page 151
Coffee

Cherry-Macaroon Layers

Almond macaroons slowly baked to a crisp are the base for this sweet sandwich.

4 egg whites
1/4 teaspoon cream of tartar
2/3 cup granulated sugar
1/3 cup powdered sugar
2 tablespoons cornstarch

1/2 teaspoon almond extract
1/2 cup blanched almonds, ground
Almond-Cheese Filling, see below
1/2 (21-oz.) can cherry-pie filling

Almond-Cheese Filling:
1 (3-oz.) pkg. cream cheese,
   room temperature
1/3 cup powdered sugar

2 tablespoons almond-flavored liqueur or
   1/2 teaspoon almond extract
1 cup whipping cream, whipped

Place egg whites in a large deep bowl. Cover with a clean cloth. Allow egg whites to warm to room temperature, 30 to 60 minutes. Preheat oven to 250F (120C). Line a baking sheet with parchment paper or plain brown paper. Draw 12 (3-inch) circles on paper; set aside. Beat egg whites and cream of tartar with an electric mixer until frothy. Gradually add granulated sugar, 1 tablespoon at a time, beating constantly. Sift together 1/3 cup powdered sugar and cornstarch. Add to egg-white mixture, 1 tablespoon at a time, beating constantly. Beat until stiff peaks form when beater is lifted from egg whites. Beat in almond extract. Fold ground nuts into egg-white mixture. Spoon into a pastry bag fitted with a large, plain tip. Pipe mixture in concentric rings, filling each circle. Or, spread macaroon mixture evenly on circles with the back of a spoon. Be sure macaroons are flat. Bake 2 hours. Turn off oven, leaving macaroons to cool in closed oven 3 to 4 hours. Remove macaroons from paper with a wide spatula. Prepare Almond-Cheese Filling. Spoon into a pastry bag fitted with a fluted tube. Turn 6 macaroons, bottom-side up, on a plate or board. Pipe a ring of Almond-Cheese Filling around edge of each macaroon. Spoon cherry-pie filling into center of ring. Top with another macaroon, bottom-side down. Decorate with remaining filling. Repeat with remaining macaroons. Refrigerate until ready to serve. Makes 6 servings.

Almond-Cheese Filling:
Combine cream cheese, powdered sugar and liqueur or extract in a medium bowl. Beat with an electric mixer until smooth. Fold in whipped cream. Set aside until ready to use.

Cherry-Dumpling Soup

Doughnut holes make easy dumplings.

1/4 cup sugar
3 tablespoons quick-cooking tapioca
1 lb. fresh or frozen, pitted, dark,
   sweet cherries

3 cups water
1/2 cup dry red wine
Cinnamon-sugar doughnut holes or
   plain doughnut holes

In a 4-quart pot, stir together sugar and tapioca. Add cherries and water. Bring to a boil over medium heat, stirring constantly. Simmer 10 minutes. Stir in wine. Ladle hot soup into individual bowls. Drop 2 doughnut holes into each bowl. Makes 4 (1-cup) servings.

How to Make Cherry-Macaroon Layers

1/Pipe egg-white mixture in concentric circles, filling each circle marked on parchment paper.

2/Pipe cream-cheese filling around edge of each macaroon. Spoon cherry filling in center. Top with another macaroon and decorate with remaining filling.

Oregon Blackberry Soup

Perfect for late summer days when the weather is hot and blackberries are ripe.

2 cups fresh or thawed frozen unsweetened blackberries	**1/2 cup blackberry preserves**
1 tablespoon lemon juice	**1 cup half and half**
1/4 cup sugar	**1/2 cup dry white wine or white grape juice**
	1 pint lemon ice cream or sherbet

Wash and hull fresh berries. Place fresh or frozen berries in a large bowl. Sprinkle lemon juice and sugar over berries; toss. Let stand 30 minutes. In another bowl, stir together preserves and half and half until blended. Stir in wine or grape juice and berries, including any juice. Cover and refrigerate until thoroughly chilled, at least 3 hours. Using a melon-baller, make 30 ice-cream or sherbet balls. Ladle cold soup into individual bowls or stemmed sherbet glasses. Top each serving with 5 ice-cream or sherbet balls. Makes 6 (1-cup) servings.

Kahlúa-Coffee Slices

Three layers of cake sandwiched with a cream-cheese and coffee filling.

Chocolate-Chip Cake, see below
1 (3-oz.) pkg. cream cheese,
  room temperature
2 tablespoons butter or margarine,
  room temperature
3 cups sifted powdered sugar

1-1/2 teaspoons instant-coffee powder
2 tablespoons boiling water
1/2 cup whipping cream
1 tablespoon Kahlúa or
  other coffee-flavored liqueur
1/2 cup chocolate-wafer cookie crumbs

Chocolate-Chip Cake:
1-1/3 cups sifted all-purpose flour
1/2 cup packed brown sugar
1/4 cup granulated sugar
2 teaspoons baking powder
1/4 teaspoon baking soda

1/2 teaspoon salt
1/3 cup shortening
2 eggs
3/4 cup milk
1/2 cup mini semisweet chocolate pieces

Prepare Chocolate-Chip Cake. Cut cooled cake in 3 (3-inch-wide) strips. Place 1 strip on a serving platter. In a medium bowl, combine cream cheese and butter or margarine. Beat with an electric mixer until smooth. Add 1 cup powdered sugar; beat until smooth. Dissolve coffee powder in boiling water. Beat into cream-cheese mixture. Add remaining powdered sugar, beating until filling is a spreading consistency. Spread generously on cake strip. Top with another strip of cake. Spread with remaining filling. Top with remaining cake strip. Beat whipping cream in a small bowl until stiff. Stir in Kahlúa or other coffee-flavored liqueur. Spread a thin layer over top and sides of cake. Use a long, wide spatula to smooth the frosting. Sprinkle cookie crumbs over top. Refrigerate until ready to serve. Makes 8 servings.

Chocolate-Chip Cake:
Preheat oven to 350F (175C). Line a 13" x 9" baking pan with waxed paper. In a large bowl, combine flour, brown sugar, granulated sugar, baking powder, baking soda, salt, shortening and eggs. Beat with an electric mixer 1 minute. Add milk; beat 2 minutes longer. Stir in chocolate pieces. Spread batter in papered pan. Be sure surface is level. Bake until a wooden pick inserted in center comes out clean, about 30 minutes. Cool cake in pan 5 minutes. Turn out cake onto a cooling rack. Peel off waxed paper. Cool completely.

Frozen Strawberry-Banana Soup

Strawberry-banana puree will keep in the freezer several weeks.

2 cups fresh strawberries
2 medium bananas, sliced
2 tablespoons lemon juice
1/2 cup water

1/4 cup sugar
1 (12-oz.) can strawberry nectar, chilled
1 (16-oz.) bottle carbonated lemon-lime soda, chilled

Set aside 6 small strawberries for garnish. Hull remaining berries. Place berries and banana slices in a blender or food processor; process until smooth. In a small saucepan, combine lemon juice, water and sugar. Stir over medium heat until sugar dissolves. Add to strawberry-banana puree. Freeze puree in an airtight container until solid. Remove from freezer. Set at room temperature 15 to 20 minutes. Break into pieces with a wooden spoon. Place pieces of frozen puree in a medium bowl. Beat with an electric mixer until smooth and slushy. Store puree in an airtight container in freezer until ready to serve. Remove puree from freezer 10 minutes before serving to allow it to soften. Combine strawberry nectar and soda in a pitcher. Using an ice-cream scoop, scoop servings of puree into stemmed sherbet glasses or bowls. Pour soda mixture around frozen puree. Garnish with whole strawberries. Serve immediately. Makes 6 (1-1/4-cup) servings.

Raspberry-Peach Bowl

Peaches are added just before serving to keep their bright color.

1 (14-oz.) pkg. frozen unsweetened
   raspberries, thawed
Water
1/4 cup sugar
1/2 cup orange juice
2 tablespoons grenadine syrup

1 cup unsweetened pineapple juice
1 tablespoon quick-cooking tapioca
2 fresh peaches or
   4 canned peach halves
1/3 cup whipping cream, whipped
2 tablespoons raspberry preserves

Drain thawed raspberries, reserving juice. Add water to juice to make 1/2 cup. Place reserved juice, sugar, orange juice, grenadine syrup, pineapple juice and tapioca in a medium saucepan; let stand 5 minutes. Bring tapioca mixture to a boil over medium heat, stirring constantly; remove from heat. Stir in raspberries. Refrigerate until well chilled, at least 4 hours. Just before serving, peel fresh peaches. Slice fresh or canned peaches. Gently fold peach slices into raspberry mixture. Ladle cold soup into individual bowls. Spoon a dollop of whipped cream onto each serving. Top cream with a spoonful of raspberry preserves. Makes 4 (1-cup) servings.

Jellied Strawberry-Swirl Soup

An unexpected flavor combination the whole family will enjoy.

2 pints fresh strawberries
1/4 cup sugar
4 cups rosé wine or cranapple juice
2 (.25-oz.) envelopes unflavored gelatin

1/2 cup cold water
3 cups buttermilk
Mint sprig, if desired

Set aside 6 berries for garnish, if desired. Wash and hull remaining berries. Slice berries top to bottom. Place berries in a bowl; sprinkle with sugar. Toss to coat berries; set aside. Heat wine or juice in a small saucepan until bubbles form around edges of pan; remove from heat. Sprinkle gelatin over cold water in a small bowl. Let stand 5 minutes to soften. Add gelatin mixture to hot wine or juice. Stir until gelatin dissolves. Refrigerate gelatin mixture until it is the consistency of unbeaten egg whites, about 1 hour. Stir in strawberries and any juice. Pour strawberry mixture into a serving bowl. Add buttermilk. Stir just enough to give a swirled effect. Refrigerate until well chilled, at least 2 hours. Garnish soup with a mint sprig or garnish each serving with reserved strawberries. Thinly slice reserved strawberries top to bottom. Spread slices at the tip in a fan shape. Place on top of each serving. Makes 6 (1-1/2-cup) servings.

Ginger-Nut Waffle Sandwich

Use a heart-shape waffle iron for an extra-fancy touch.

4 Gingerbread Waffles, see below
1/2 cup whipping cream
1 tablespoon maple syrup or
   maple-flavored syrup

1 (1-pint) block maple-nut ice cream
8 pecan halves or walnut halves

Gingerbread Waffles:
2 eggs
1/2 cup packed brown sugar
1/2 cup butter or margarine, melted
1/4 cup molasses
1/4 cup milk

1-1/2 cups sifted all-purpose flour
2 teaspoons baking powder
1/4 teaspoon salt
1/2 teaspoon ground ginger
1/2 teaspoon ground cinnamon

Prepare Gingerbread Waffles. Cut each waffle into 4 pieces. Beat whipping cream in a small bowl until stiff peaks form. Stir in maple syrup. Cut ice cream into slices to fit waffles. Top half the waffles with an ice-cream slice. Place remaining waffles on top. Place whipped cream in a pastry bag fitted with a star tip. Pipe a star of whipped cream on top of each waffle sandwich, or spoon a dollop of cream on top. Press pecan or walnut halves into cream. Makes 8 servings.

Gingerbread Waffles:
Preheat waffle iron according to manufacturer's directions. Beat eggs and brown sugar in a large bowl with an electric mixer until smooth and slightly thickened. In another bowl, combine butter or margarine, molasses and milk. Sift together flour, baking powder, salt, ginger and cinnamon. Stir half the molasses mixture into egg mixture. Add half the flour mixture; stir until combined. Repeat adding molasses and flour mixtures alternately. Do not overmix. Cook waffles according to manufacturer's directions. Cool waffles on a rack.

Jellied Strawberry-Swirl Soup

Cherry-Chocolate Alaska Layers

An elegant dessert for special occasions.

Chocolate Cake, see below
1 (1-pint) block dark-cherry ice cream
3 egg whites

1/4 teaspoon cream of tartar
1/3 cup sugar
2 teaspoons unsweetened cocoa

Chocolate Cake:
3 tablespoons butter or margarine,
  room temperature
1/2 cup sugar
1 egg
3/4 cup sifted all-purpose flour

1/2 teaspoon baking soda
1/4 teaspoon salt
4-1/2 teaspoons unsweetened cocoa
1/2 cup buttermilk

Prepare Chocolate Cake. Cut cooled cake in half, making 2 (8" x 4") rectangles. Place 1 cake layer on an ovenproof serving plate. Cut ice-cream block in half lengthwise. Arrange ice cream so it covers cake without extending beyond cake edges. Top with remaining cake layer. Place cake in freezer while preparing meringue. Preheat oven to 450F (230C). In a large bowl, beat egg whites and cream of tartar until frothy. In a small bowl, stir together sugar and cocoa. Sprinkle sugar mixture over egg whites, 1 teaspoon at a time, while beating. Beat until stiff peaks form. Spread meringue over cake sandwich in a swirling motion, taking care to cover cake and ice cream completely with meringue. Bake cake until lightly browned, 3 to 5 minutes. Makes 6 servings.

Chocolate Cake:
Preheat oven to 350F (175C). Line an 8-inch-square baking pan with waxed paper. Combine butter or margarine, sugar and egg in a medium bowl. Beat with an electric mixer until light and fluffy. Sift together flour, baking soda, salt and cocoa. Add flour mixture to egg mixture. Beat only until combined. Add buttermilk; beat again until combined. Spread batter in prepared pan. Bake until a wooden pick inserted in center comes out clean, about 30 minutes. Cool in pan 5 minutes. Turn out cake onto a rack. Peel off waxed paper. Cool cake.

Variation
Substitute 1 (9-ounce) package chocolate-cake mix for Chocolate Cake. Prepare batter following package directions. Bake in an 8-inch-square pan.

Paradise Wedges

Pineapple, coconut and peanuts make plain white bread taste as good as cake.

1 (3-oz.) pkg. cream cheese,
  room temperature
2 tablespoons powdered sugar
1/2 cup drained crushed pineapple
1/4 teaspoon grated lemon peel
1 teaspoon lemon juice

4 slices soft white bread
1/2 cup shredded coconut
1/2 cup finely chopped peanuts
1 egg
2 tablespoons milk

Preheat oven to 375F (190C). Grease a baking sheet. In a small bowl, beat cream cheese and powdered sugar until smooth. Stir in pineapple, lemon peel and lemon juice. Trim crust from bread. Spread 2 slices generously with pineapple filling. Top each with another slice of bread. Cut sandwiches diagonally corner to corner, making 4 triangles. Combine coconut and peanuts on a sheet of waxed paper. In a pie plate, stir egg and milk with a fork until combined. Dip all sides of sandwiches in egg mixture. Roll in coconut mixture. Press coconut mixture onto sandwiches. Place sandwiches on greased baking sheet. Bake until lightly browned, about 10 minutes. Turn over and bake 5 minutes longer. Cool slightly. Serve warm or at room temperature. Makes 4 servings.

Scandinavian Fruit Soup

Originally a winter favorite made from dried fruit and served warm.

1 (8-oz.) pkg. mixed dried fruit
1/2 cup red wine
3-1/2 cups water
1 cinnamon stick
2 whole cloves
1/4 teaspoon ground cardamom

1 tablespoon cornstarch
1/4 cup cold water
1 (21-oz.) can cherry-pie filling
1 tablespoon lemon juice
1 (8-oz.) carton spiced-apple- or
  lemon-flavored yogurt (1 cup)

Place dried fruit in a large saucepan. Add red wine and water. Let stand 30 minutes. Add cinnamon stick, cloves and cardamom. Bring to a boil; reduce heat. Cover and simmer 20 minutes. In a small bowl, combine cornstarch and cold water, stirring until smooth. Pour cornstarch mixture in a thin stream into soup, stirring constantly. Cook until thickened, stirring constantly. Add cherry-pie filling and lemon juice. Serve soup warm or cold. To serve cold, refrigerate soup until well chilled, at least 2 hours. Top each bowl of warm or cold soup with a dollop of yogurt. Makes 6 (1-cup) servings.

Strawberry Ribbons

Ribbons of nutty pastry filled with strawberry cream.

Nut Pastry, see below
1/2 cup sifted powdered sugar
1 tablespoon hot water
1 (10-oz.) pkg. frozen sweetened
   strawberries, thawed
2 egg whites

1 cup whipping cream
2 pints fresh strawberries
   (about 26 berries)
2 tablespoons strawberry jam
Mint sprigs, if desired

Nut Pastry:
1/4 cup nuts such as slivered almonds,
   walnuts, pecans or macadamia nuts
1-1/2 cups sifted all-purpose flour

1/2 teaspoon salt
1/2 cup shortening
3 to 4 tablespoons cold water

Prepare Nut Pastry. Preheat oven to 375F (190C). On a floured board, roll out pastry to a 12'' x 8'' rectangle. Trim edges straight. Place rectangle on a baking sheet. Prick the surface with tines of a fork. Using the dull side of a large knife, make a lengthwise indentation in the center of the pastry, running the entire length of the rectangle. Bake until pastry is lightly browned, about 10 minutes. Cool pastry. Cut completely cooled pastry along indentation. In a small bowl, combine powdered sugar and hot water. Beat until smooth to form a glaze. Spread glaze over half the pastry. Drain frozen strawberries, reserving syrup. Pour syrup into a small saucepan. Bring to a boil; remove from heat. In a medium bowl, beat egg whites until soft peaks form. Slowly pour hot syrup, in a thin stream, over egg whites while beating. Add thawed strawberries. Continue beating until soft peaks form. In another bowl, beat whipping cream until stiff peaks form. Fold whipped cream into strawberry mixture. Select 3 of the most perfect fresh strawberries; set aside. Wash remaining berries; hull. Trim hulled end of 16 to 24 berries so they are about equal in length. Place unglazed piece of pastry on a serving plate. Arrange 8 to 12 trimmed strawberries, with tips up, in a row along each long side of pastry. Spoon enough strawberry mixture between rows of strawberries barely to cover tips of berries. Place glazed pastry piece on top, glazed-side up. Spread remaining strawberry mixture around sides. Cut reserved strawberries in half, top to bottom. Do not hull berries. Place berry halves on waxed paper. Spoon jam over each. Refrigerate pastry and glazed berries at least 4 hours before serving. Place berry halves in a row along length of pastry. Garnish with mint sprigs, if desired. Use a serrated knife to cut between each berry half. Makes 6 servings.

Nut Pastry:
Finely chop nuts in a blender or food processor. Combine nuts, flour and salt in a medium bowl. Cut in 1/4 cup shortening with a pastry blender until mixture resembles cornmeal. Cut in remaining shortening until it is in pea-size pieces. Sprinkle water over flour mixture, 1 teaspoon at a time, while tossing mixture with a fork. Continue adding water until mixture begins to hold together. Form dough into a ball.

How to Make Strawberry Ribbons

1/Arrange strawberries along each long side of pastry. Spoon strawberry mixture between rows of strawberries.

2/Top with glazed pastry piece. Spread remaining strawberry mixture around sides. To serve, place glazed strawberries on pastry.

Chilled Pumpkin Bisque

An easy dessert that kids can make.

1 (17-oz.) can solid-packed pumpkin
1/4 cup sugar
1 teaspoon ground cinnamon
1/2 teaspoon salt
1/2 teaspoon ground ginger
1/4 teaspoon ground cloves

1/4 teaspoon ground nutmeg
1 qt. milk (4 cups)
1 (3-3/4-oz.) pkg. instant butterscotch-
     pudding mix
1 cup pecan-cookie crumbs

In a large bowl, combine pumpkin, sugar, cinnamon, salt, ginger, cloves and nutmeg. Stir until blended. Add milk and pudding mix. Beat with a whisk or rotary beater until mixture thickens. Refrigerate until well chilled, at least 2 hours. To serve, ladle into individual bowls. Sprinkle cookie crumbs over each serving. Makes 6 (1-cup) servings.

Marshmallow-Iced Brownies

Freezing this brownie and ice-cream sandwich makes eating easier.

1-1/2 cups sifted all-purpose flour
1 teaspoon baking powder
1/8 teaspoon salt
1/2 cup butter or margarine
2 oz. unsweetened chocolate
1-1/2 cups sugar

2 eggs
1 teaspoon vanilla extract
1/2 cup chopped walnuts or pecans
18 large marshmallows, cut in halves
2 (1-pint) blocks ice cream, such as
    fudge ripple, neopolitan or banana

Preheat oven to 350F (175C). Grease a 13" x 9" baking pan. Sift flour with baking powder and salt. Melt butter or margarine and chocolate in a medium saucepan over low heat; remove from heat. Stir until smooth. Stir in sugar, eggs and vanilla until smooth. Add flour mixture and nuts; stir until blended. Spread batter into prepared pan. Bake until a wooden pick inserted in center comes out clean, about 20 minutes. Cool brownies in pan. When completely cool, cut brownies in 3 strips lengthwise. Cut each strip in 6 pieces crosswise. Remove brownies from pan. Preheat broiler. Arrange 9 brownies on a baking sheet. Place 4 pieces marshmallow on each brownie. Place brownies under broiler until marshmallows toast and melt; cool. Cut ice cream into 9 slices. Top each marshmallow-covered brownie with an ice-cream slice. Place a plain brownie on top. Wrap each sandwich in plastic wrap. Freeze until solid, at least 4 hours. Makes 9 servings.

Apple Chimichangas

Apple pie Mexican-style!

8 cups sliced, peeled, tart green apples
    (about 4 large)
3/4 cup granulated sugar
1 tablespoon all-purpose flour
1/2 teaspoon ground cinnamon
1/3 cup raisins
1/4 cup chopped walnuts

6 (10-inch) flour tortillas
1/4 cup butter or margarine
2 tablespoons brown sugar
1/4 cup dry white wine
Powdered sugar
1 cup whipping cream, if desired

Place apple slices in a 3-quart saucepan. In a small bowl, combine granulated sugar, flour and cinnamon; stir until blended. Sprinkle sugar mixture over apples; stir gently. Cover and cook over low heat, stirring frequently, until apples are tender, 20 to 30 minutes. Add raisins and nuts; stir. Remove from heat. Preheat oven to 350F (175C). Wrap tortillas in foil. Warm in oven until softened, about 10 minutes. Place about 1/2 cup apple filling in center of a warm tortilla. Fold 1 side over filling, folding tortilla almost in half. Fold in 2 sides envelope fashion. Roll up folded tortilla. Repeat with remaining tortillas and apple filling. In a large skillet, melt butter or margarine. Add brown sugar and wine. Stir until sugar dissolves. Bring to a boil. Place filled tortillas in boiling syrup. Cook 2 minutes on each side, turning only once. Place chimichangas on serving platter. Sift powdered sugar over top. Serve with cream to pour over chimichangas, if desired. Makes 6 servings.

Index

Index

Index

Index

5.726904884138